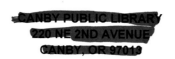
# Storytime and Beyond

D1601950

# Storytime and Beyond

## Having Fun with Early Literacy

Kathy Barco and Melanie Borski-Howard

LIBRARIES
UNLIMITED™
An Imprint of ABC-CLIO, LLC
Santa Barbara, California • Denver, Colorado

**Library of Congress Cataloging-in-Publication Data**

Names: Barco, Kathy, 1946– author. | Borski-Howard, Melanie, author.
Title: Storytime and beyond : having fun with early literacy / Kathy Barco
    and Melanie Borski-Howard.
Description: Santa Barbara, California : Libraries Unlimited, [2018] | Includes
    bibliographical references and index.
Identifiers: LCCN 2018017819 (print) | LCCN 2018026916 (ebook) |
    ISBN 9781440858994 (ebook) | ISBN 9781440858987 (paperback)
Subjects: LCSH: Storytelling. | Language arts (Early childhood) | Libraries and
    preschool children.
Classification: LCC LB1140.35.S76 (ebook) | LCC LB1140.35.S76 B37 2018 (print) |
    DDC 372.67/7—dc23
LC record available at https://lccn.loc.gov/2018017819

ISBN: 978-1-4408-5898-7 (paperback)
        978-1-4408-5899-4 (ebook)

22  21  20  19  18    1  2  3  4  5

This book is also available as an eBook.

Libraries Unlimited
An Imprint of ABC-CLIO, LLC

ABC-CLIO, LLC
130 Cremona Drive, P.O. Box 1911
Santa Barbara, California 93116-1911
www.abc-clio.com

This book is printed on acid-free paper ∞

Manufactured in the United States of America

To Kristina "Krissie" Carter, youth services librarian at the
Clovis-Carver Public Library from 2002 to 2017. You were a
positive influence in so many lives. RIP
—KB

To my incredibly supportive coworker, Alice Eccles,
who has been by my side doing musical storytimes since
the program began.
—MBH

# Contents

# Introduction

Welcome to *Storytime and Beyond: Having Fun with Literacy*! You're in for a bonanza of fun.

Are you a children's librarian or teacher/parent/grandparent/family/caregiver of children getting ready to read? Do you work as a literacy coach or counselor with older youngsters and even adults who need literacy motivation? Most of all, are you someone who is interested in opening up the world of books to those who may not yet have discovered it? YOU should explore this book!

Often literacy is considered the job of librarians and teachers. But parents, families, and other caregivers are almost always a child's first teachers. They lay the first foundation of reading by reading to their children. Bedtime stories are crucial, but word games, songs, and lullabies are equally valuable. How many youngsters learn their alphabet by singing along with someone else? For sure, librarians and teachers *do* literacy—you could even call them literacy *gurus*—but anyone can get into the act, and in on the fun, too. (NOTE: Singing is one of the five Every Child Ready to Read (ECRR) practices. Read a full description of ECRR in Melanie's Chapter 4 "Musical Storytimes Build Literacy Skills.")

What can you expect to find inside our enticing orange cover? There's something useful, interesting, creative, and above all, *fun* in every chapter. Whether you read straight through or just dip into the various sections, you may frequently find yourself thinking, "I could do that!"

The main title really sums it up: *Storytime and Beyond*. Storytimes are a way of life for children's librarians and for many parents/grandparents/caregivers who faithfully bring their kids to the library. And this book is packed with tips, scripts, bibliographies, statistics, and anecdotes that relate directly to storytimes. But there's a lot of literacy to be picked up after storytime is over. Reinforcing storytime events at home or in another setting contributes to the original experience. There are many *other* ways to enhance literacy. And they're painless (and *fun*)!

Here's a quick look at what you will find in the following six chapters. (Note: the authors went halfsies . . . Kathy wrote the first three chapters and Melanie did Chapters 4, 5, and 6. But this is *not* a numbers book! Maybe if they do a sequel . . .)

## CHAPTER 1: ALL I REALLY NEED TO KNOW I LEARNED FROM ABC BOOKS

Speaking of fun and painless . . . alphabet books are a terrific way to strengthen literacy. They can be used with almost any age, are fascinating to look at, come in a wide variety of topics, and inspire questions and conversations, thus exercising talking skills. Older youngsters and adults who have struggled with reading might be offended by what they might consider "baby or kiddie" alphabet books, but they would love spending time with some of the specialized ABC books that seemingly involve the alphabet almost incidentally.

Kathy read over 250 ABC books as background for this chapter. She describes how alphabet books can be invaluable keys to spark interest in readers of all ages. Get ready to amble through the alphabet via 26 ABC Mini-Adventures that start with Q for Quilt (the struggle and reasoning behind bringing Q to the top of the list explains how readers might compile their own ABC Mini-Adventures). Kathy had fun naming each of the Adventures. For example: J is for Juravenator, K is for Strikeout, R is for Read It Again and Again!, and U is for Underpants. Fun, huh? As she says, this is probably the closest she'll ever get to write an ABC book of her own!

In case you're wondering, she doesn't include all 250+ ABC books she read for research. But nearly 100 titles are described in various Adventures. They also appear in the bibliography at the end of the chapter. Kathy includes a photo of the first ABC Book she ever had: *The Jolly Jump-Ups ABC Book* by Geraldine Clyne, published in 1948. It's still in great shape, considering that it's a pop-up book.

The chapter details enrichment activities and tips on how ABC books can cater to a reader's personal interests. There is also a list of "selling points" with ideas on where to find used/bargain ABC books, taking advantage of puzzles or mysteries built into the books, class activities where each child has a different alphabet book, using the books with ESL students, and a cure for an ABC book addiction.

# CHAPTER 2: LITERACY DOODADS: NOT JUST LETTER MAGNETS ON THE REFRIGERATOR ANYMORE!

First things first: What is a *Doodad*? They do exist, right? . . . Right! Kathy devotes an entire chapter to them. We can infer from the title that letter magnets must be mere components in a well-equipped doodad caboodle. (A caboodle, by the way, is a group, bunch, lot, pack, or collection of things or people.) See her extensive description of what constitutes a doodad at the beginning of the chapter.

As she states, letter magnets are attractive in many ways (the refrigerator . . . *and beyond!*). See how many of these uses have occurred to you! Starting with the alphabet magnets and throughout this chapter, Kathy includes three types of bulleted material:

- Book Suggestions
- ➢ Literacy Activities
- ✓ Doodad Factoids—assorted comments

The first of the four books she suggests that feature alphabet magnets is *The Shivers in the Fridge* by Fran Manushkin, illustrated by Paul O. Zelinsky. The book's cover was her inspiration for the title of this chapter. All the books that are cited are included in the bibliography at the end of Chapter 2. This chapter also features plenty of photos. These actually cut down on your reading time, though, if you consider that a picture is worth a thousand words.

Balloon letters are star players in Kathy's repertoire of doodads. In this circumstance, inflation is a *good* thing. Balloons are perfect ice-breakers when speaking to an audience of parents or caregivers who may be reluctant to take part in a group activity. Kathy's "Balloon Etiquette" gives hints for conducting a balloon event of your own. Follow her tips and you won't blow it! (Or maybe, you will!)

Shoelaces, yarn, pipe cleaners, chopsticks, and even Jenga game pieces become doodads in the right hands (ideally, a child's).

Caution: you might want to have a snack before sampling the **Food!** suggestions. On the menu are alphabet cookies, alphabet soup, alphabet cereal, and alphabet pasta, to mention just a few. Plenty of book suggestions, literacy activities, and doodad factoids appear as well. Warning: you may find yourself putting aside this book and heading straight to the kitchen after you read the section on Pancake Letters.

Have you ever thought of posters and placemats as literacy doodads? As part of a child's environment, either at home, in the library, or at school, these items showcase the alphabet passively, but they make a subtle impression. Wallpapering an entire room with an ABC pattern might be a little extreme, but a wall or shelf displaying a child's initials in various forms (wood, metal, plastic, foam, etc.) would gently reinforce their identity and raise their self-esteem.

Initials and monograms are popular design features we come across daily. Kathy describes an idea lifted from illuminated manuscripts that could provide a starting point for several literacy activities. Thanks to Google Images and Pinterest, examples are available for this and almost everything that Kathy alludes to in this chapter. Think back to some of the earliest fairy tale books you encountered. Didn't the stories often begin or end with a fancy "dropped cap" letter? "Once upon a time . . . And they lived happily ever after . . ." You're visualizing a fancy O and A, right?

Did you have a "scribble slate" as a child? You wrote on it with a stylus. Everything magically disappeared when the plastic cover sheet was lifted up. Such toys are still made today. These, along with chalk boards and dry-erase boards, are inexpensive, reusable, and reliable ways for youngsters to practice scribbling and eventually forming letters. Along the way, a child develops small muscle coordination (holding the stylus, chalk, or dry-erase marker). In addition, two of the ECRR practices are covered: writing and letter knowledge. *Fun*, and *painless*. (Melanie gives a full description of ECRR in Chapter 4.)

The power of the chalkboard is charmingly conveyed in Kathy's first "Doodad Anecdote." *Wheel of Fortune* fans will appreciate having yet another justification for watching the show! "Honey, it's work-related!"

Pizza was the theme of her most successful storytime throughout her career. She gave it countless times in various libraries and demonstrated it during workshops and presentations. Find her pizza storytime "recipe" in the section on puzzles.

Scrabble letters, alphabet blocks, stencils, rubber stamps, flashcards, and scrapbook paper are doodad material. The entry about stickers contains a cautionary tale that Kathy hopes will save readers possible embarrassment and help avoid stress in children. Don't miss that!

Can a *book* be a doodad? In the case of *I Spy ABC: Totally Crazy Letters!*, the answer is YES! Find out how under the heading "**ABC Books Themselves!**" If you manage to get your hands on a copy of this book, be prepared to get lost in it. And good luck getting it back from anyone you show it to, adults especially! If you've ever wondered what to do with that drawer full of postage stamps, or the jar of buttons that belonged to your great aunt, or those matchbox cars just too precious to part with . . . here's your answer. And literacy is involved!

The main thing to keep in mind with all these literacy doodads is to have *fun*. In addition, whatever doodad you're using, be sure to stop when the child is still intensely interested. They'll be more eager to do it again . . . but *later on*. Also, you don't have to make a major investment in doodads. Many of the ones Kathy includes can be do-it-yourself craft projects in the library, classroom, or home. Making them together involves yet another ECRR practice: talking!

Kathy's last doodad anecdote describes an outreach visit she made to the Bernalillo County Metropolitan Detention Facility. If you needed any more justification for the importance of literacy, you'll find it here. (See Melanie's Chapter 6 "Outreach Storytimes," for descriptions of several other types of outreach.)

# CHAPTER 3: DYNAMIC DISPLAYS: MINIMUM WORK, MAXIMUM IMPACT

Are you a fairly new librarian wondering why they didn't offer Displays 101 in Library School? Or maybe you've been in a library for a while and are looking for fresh ideas to help you fill a bare bulletin board and some empty display cases? Perhaps you're a teacher looking for some literacy-based ideas to put on the wall or door? As a parent, grandparent, or caregiver, have you ever noticed displays in libraries, and wondered how they might impact your youngster (or yourself)?

Displays contribute to literacy in many ways, and often those ways are so subtle that a viewer might not even realize that learning is taking place. (Actually, that's a good thing, if you subscribe to the theory that literacy should be painless and *fun*!)

Themed displays based on various days, weeks, or months turn up every year. They're right there on the calendar: National Pancake Day, Black History Month, Read Across

America Week, Breast Cancer Awareness Month, National Library Week, National Donut Day, Poetry Month, and so on.

Books are a reliable focus for displays. These usually follow a theme, too. Mysteries, puzzle books, holidays, works by authors whose birthdays fall in the month, books on cooking, travel, crafts, specific states or countries . . . your choice! An easy February display can contain books with red covers. This is quick and easy to do by plucking likely candidates right off the shelves. As the books are checked out, new ones can easily be found to replace them, and practically any staff member can add a few just by browsing the shelves or even looking over newly returned items. Orange books might be featured in October. Maybe *Storytime and Beyond* will turn up in someone's October display! (Of course, it will be checked out *immediately* . . .)

Starting with her very first library job, Kathy has enjoyed doing displays. And luckily for us, she had the foresight to take photographs. She started with a camera that required film (!) but has kept up with technology through digital photography (still with a camera and memory cards) up to the present with her ever-present phone. (Note to reader: if you don't already snap pix of your displays, start doing it!)

They will come in handy at future job interviews, add zip to presentations, and jog your memory when you can't recall what you put up for Groundhog Day last year! By the way, Kathy is still doing displays. She was invited to re-create her popular Curious George display at one of her former libraries. You may be curious about George . . . in graduate school Kathy did her master's project on that good little monkey. Afterwards, friends showered her with Curious George items, which, in fact, could probably qualify as doodads! George is a super friend of literacy! Kathy's collection could probably fill several cases by now. Characters from children's literature are popular display case subjects. (See references to Alice in Wonderland and Dr. Seuss cases below.)

If you agree with the earlier statement that pictures are worth a thousand words, you'll be amazed to know that this chapter holds at least 10,000, not counting the surrounding text! Whether you're trying to fill a problem area on a wall or a mega-gallon aquarium tank donated by a generous patron (who didn't include the fish and accompanying paraphernalia), you'll find some interesting, fun, and easy tricks in this chapter. Are you trying to cope with a wall that contains a nasty stain/dent/crack and repairing it doesn't fit into the budget? Consider it a challenge to your creativity! Of course, you could just slap a poster up there . . . but read this chapter before you resort to that.

The examples Kathy showcases (see what she did there?) are meant to inspire you to devise your own displays. The items she uses as "filler" in a case to draw roving eyes are like a carnival barker. Snappy patter in the form of sparkly stuff (sequins, glitter, shiny objects) serves as the "hook" to draw in the spectators. Once they're by the display, their eyes roam to the main attraction. Sneaky, right? Effective? *You bet*!

The step-by-step descriptions of items she has used in various cases are designed to gently encourage you to try new things. Details of her Alice in Wonderland I Spy case, and the ever-popular Dr. Seuss case (she did it several years in a row) provide a formula for assembling a dynamic display.

You might think that displays are supposed to be informative, fun, nonthreatening, enticing, attractive to all ages, and just plain harmless. You might rethink that idea after reading Kathy's account of a challenge to a publication that was part of an array of Halloween books.

If you're in a branch library (or not!), branch out into a tree display that is "evergreen" (functional through more than one growing season). Some of the lettering techniques appearing in the accompanying photos may look dated, corny, old-fashioned, or low-tech. But they can also be viewed as *vintage* or even *retro* . . . highly desirable characteristics in some circles. Seasonal changes are easy, thanks to the tips Kathy includes.

Several photos and a lot of description explain another very basic wall display that lasted for over six months with minimal changes (thus, minimal work!). See how some very "cookie-cutter" gingerbread folks skipped through the seasons from late November up until Summer Reading Program took over. Several years later these smart cookies turned up as "Ninja-Bread Heroes" for several super-hero-themed events. Kathy calls the section just described, "If you give a mouse a (gingerbread) cookie, she'll want to decorate it (again and again)!" This is a play on the words in the titles of a beloved children's series written by Laura Numeroff with delightful illustrations by Felicia Bond. There are several references to Numeroff's books in Kathy's chapters. The basic formula is "If you give a [blank] a [blank] . . ." which is completed with "then they'll ask for a [blank] to go with it." Starting with a cookie, a muffin, a pancake, even a donut, Numeroff's stories roll along. This template could be used with a youngster, asking them to fill in the blanks. You're probably thinking of ways *you* would fill them in! If Kathy were to write a book in this vein (as an *almost* native New Mexican), it would probably be "If you give a roadrunner a *sopapilla*, she'll ask for some honey to go with it." And there would be an illustration of a bear-shaped honey dispenser.

This chapter concludes with an anecdote about how a seemingly inconsequential item in her "Day of the Dead/*Día de los Muertos*" display case may have sparked a medical career.

**

Do you hear what I hear? It's the sound of music! Here comes Melanie with her guitar. The library is alive with the sound of music (for the next three chapters!).

# CHAPTER 4: MUSICAL STORYTIMES BUILD LITERACY SKILLS

Melanie starts out on a positive *note*, by saying she hopes to inspire storytellers to incorporate a musical instrument into their storytimes. Spoiler alert: She provides *tons* of inspiration! That alone should be enough to convince you to skip the rest of the "Introduction" and go straight to her chapters. But that would be like just hearing the first few measures of an overture and fast-forwarding ahead to the other movements. Or, if you prefer an analogy that spotlights *singing*, that would be like listening the first few notes of an aria and skipping ahead to the finale with the massed chorus.

Be advised: Melanie uses anecdotes. A lot of anecdotes. And they're warm and informative. Just like a good story. And *story* is the first part of the first word in the title of this book. Everyone loves stories. Storytimes feature stories! Who can resist? Melanie sums up her storytime philosophy in her very first paragraphs. But, as they say, the best is yet to come.

We learn about her background: education, early library jobs, and her strong attraction to musical theater. (How many librarians feel they're in *showbiz*, up there in front of an audience of adoring kids and parents? More about that later on . . .)

We go along on the 15- to 20-year journey as Melanie progresses from having no music in storytime, through adding some songs, to (currently) including her guitar in every storytime. Speaking of showbiz, she blames (make that *gives credit to*) Woody Guthrie. Her description of his influence includes the fact that she cried through her rendition of *This Land Is Your Land.* Apparently, she *still* cries through some songs. But that's fine. How many librarians have cried when reading a story? Perhaps one that their mother read to them as a child. They can still hear *her* voice when they read it. Is there such a story that tugs at *your* heartstrings?

Speaking of strings, Melanie had to pull a few strings when she asked her manager to allow another person to be brought in to share in the musical storytime *fun* (not to mention the *work* too—these gigs are far from easy, especially when you start attracting big audiences!). Melanie and Alice: how's that for a dynamic duo! We're talking three figures here! Would you love to welcome that kind of crowds into your library for storytime? Do you have the necessary space? And more important: Would your local fire marshal mind?

Still speaking of strings, Melanie didn't even *have* a guitar when all this began. They were using toy instruments! But then, as she says, "Something magical happened: a coworker donated her guitar to the library!" You're probably saying "and the rest is history." Not exactly. Melanie didn't just pick up that donated guitar and start singin' and strummin' her way into the hearts of hundreds. Her account of how she learned how to play (with help from her guitar-playin' husband, many YouTube tutorials, and lots and lots of practice) could be the basis for a nifty children's book!

It wasn't until 2012 that Melanie *dared* (her word) to play her guitar in her musical storytimes. Further along in this chapter we discover the evolution of weekly storytimes and the addition of Ruth the ukulele player.

Now that you know how this all got started, Melanie discusses how to create and present a musical storytime—in particular, how to incorporate instruments to make it extra fun! She provides information on ECRR, an early literacy program developed in 2004 by the Public Library Association and the Association for Library Services to Children, two groups within the American Library Association. As she states, "Before creating any early literacy storytime, you need information, so you can make informed decisions about choosing materials. I am very thankful for ECRR and the wealth of knowledge it gives to educators and caregivers." She gives extensive information about ECRR components, including the Six Skills and Five Practices. These may be familiar to many librarians reading this book. If not, they form a sound basis for early literacy instruction that can be understood and used by anyone: parents/grandparents/caregivers, teachers, literacy coaches, and anyone who understands the importance of literacy and is interested in fostering it.

Melanie believes three things are necessary for preparing a successful musical storytime: (1) choose books and flannels that are musically based, (2) incorporate instruments and let children experience them hands-on, and (3) have two storytellers present the storytimes. A combo of text and photos expands this framework. She lists appropriate books and includes flannels, fingerplays, and songs for a variety of storytimes that could be patterns for anyone to use as is or modify based on their own circumstances, collections, and level of expertise. As if this weren't enough, she also provides great details in sections such as "It's All about the Books," "Incorporating Instruments," and "Presenting with a Partner."

By now, you're probably itching to start humming along with Melanie. This chapter includes documentation on why music is important in early literacy, more about the Six Practices and Five Skills of ECRR (with terrific examples!), and plenty of research and firsthand experiences. There are websites mentioned, and the references at the end of the chapter provide a door into so much more.

She concludes the chapter "I have children in my storytime that speak other languages and many that are just developing those words to communicate. Music and rhythm are something they all are drawn to from day one. From the beating of their mother's heart, to the rhythms they hear every day, to the songs that fill their souls. It is nourishment—and essential for me and my passion for early literacy."

Anyone tearing up? Put away those hankies! There are several more verses to this song!

# CHAPTER 5: THEMED STORYTIMES AND SCRIPTS

Have you ever been in a jam, needing to come up with a last-minute storytime? Speaking of jam, this chapter is jammed with actual scripts from musical storytimes with Ruth and Melanie, during which they use instruments and music. Imagine having a set of blueprints for perfect musical storytimes, plus an Ikea-style kit of components to put it together. The good news is that those kits are *here*! The *better* news is that the how-to-build-it instructions are super-easy to understand. The *best* news is that these storytimes promote literacy . . . *and they're fun!*

If you enjoyed the food-related literacy doodads in Chapter 2, you'll devour the food-themed musical storytimes: *Fruits and Veggies* and *Pizza and Ice Cream*. Songs, fingerplays, flannels, and imaginative play are described in exhaustive detail. Alternates are often suggested in case you are unfamiliar with a certain book or song or have something already in your collection you prefer to use.

Speaking of jam *again*, one of several books mentioned in "Food: Fruits and Veggies" is *Jamberry* by Bruce Degen. Body motions for the presenter to model when doing the Banana Dance are spelled out: put arms over head, sweep arms down, and so on. A flannel: A-P-P-L-E, is a Ruth-modified version of "Bingo Was His Name-O." Melanie's "embarrassing side story" falls into the category of hilarious anecdotes and/or situations many librarians can identify with.

As mentioned before, this storytime features the words and movements to the Banana Dance. And if you just can't visualize this . . . be patient. All will become clear!

As an alternative to the healthy characteristics of Fruits and Veggies, order up Pizza and Ice Cream. Other themes covered in this section include Love, Peacefulness, and Emotions, and . . . Pollinators. This one includes a real blast from the past, for Melanie at least, and anyone who grew up watching *Sesame Street* (*like she did!*). It's a combination of flannel/ song on guitar: "Ladybug's Picnic." Melanie laments that presenting it made her feel old: not one of the caregivers in the audience knew the song!

Several librarians do blogs about storytimes. Melanie even considered doing one herself . . . *briefly*. "I didn't feel young and hip enough!" she confides. But in an event reminiscent of the donated guitar, Channel 8, Boulder's local television station, asked if the library would be willing to let Melanie and the staff film some of their storytimes. "Walla!" exults Melanie. Here was a perfect way to document some of the things they had been doing! They began filming in 2016.

Melanie describes the two main issues they discovered with filming storytimes: (1) Finding materials and making sure to have permission for use from the performer and/or publisher and (2) filming storytimes and finding an audience. Does the thought of contacting publishing companies for copyright permission regarding books sound daunting? Melanie's sample template is provided in this chapter.

Actually, this chapter could be summed up as follows: it's a handbook/songbook/ textbook/poetry anthology.

- *Hand* motions and fingerplays are provided.
- *Songs* burst from the pages.
- *Text* fills in the spaces.
- *Poetry* abounds.

Practically everything you ever wanted to know about doing storytimes is here, plus lots of great information you didn't even know that you didn't know. You may remember an earlier reference to librarians and "showbiz." Hang onto your seats. Melanie provides four complete "Read with Us" storytime scripts. These seem a little bare-bones at first, maybe even sparse with things like song, book, activity, book, book, song, song, activity, song/

dance. But wait! She also provides the URL for hearing and seeing the storytimes filmed and broadcast by Channel 8, Boulder, Colorado. Viewing these can best be compared to the slogan for the Mounds candy bar: *Indescribably Delicious*!

Nobody would blame you if you *really did put down this book right now*, went to a computer or your phone, and brought up an episode of "Read with Us."

As of press time of this book, there were 12 episodes online. These are invaluable for beginning librarians, teachers, and veteran librarians looking for new or fresh ways to enhance storytimes. A caregiver or perhaps a homeschooler could share these with youngsters, and it would be *almost* as good as going to a live storytime at a library. Endless possibilities: interactions with real children, fielding their questions, expert use of puppets, a relaxed style, and more . . . these shows are a master class in Storytime. And, as promised, you will see Melanie and Alice doing the Banana Dance!

Assuming you can resist the urge to binge-watch "Read with Us," this jam-packed chapter contains fascinating descriptions and examples of toddler storytimes, storytimes where caregivers are present, and sensory storytimes, which cater to children living on the autism spectrum.

But . . . if you are helplessly drawn back to "Read with Us," there is a show-stopping version of "The Itsy-Bitsy Spider" about midway through Episode 10. You'll never do it the "old way" again!

# CHAPTER 6: OUTREACH STORYTIMES

Have you ever been surprised while out in public to see someone that you've only ever encountered in a specific place? Librarians (and teachers) deal with this regularly. "Wait a minute, don't you live at the *library*?" said a three-year old who spotted Melanie at the grocery store.

Think of this as yet one more reason to bring the library to the community. A good subtitle for this chapter would be: "Taking Storytime on the Road!"

Here Melanie highlights what she has learned from going out of her comfort zone: the library. She explains why it was hard for her "as a librarian/introvert." But leaving that comfort zone really improved her confidence as a storyteller and made her appreciate her job as a librarian.

Right away, the Facebook group, Storytime Underground, receives a shout out from Melanie. She and Kathy are followers of the 10,000+-member group, as well as frequent contributors. It is an excellent resource.

This chapter discusses a variety of outreach opportunities. In addition, it provides insight into doing storytimes as a freelancer (not as a part of a library job).

Melanie differentiates a library storytime from a preschool storytime. The location is not the library, for starters. Also, parents and caregivers (aside from preschool staff, who may not be involved in the activity at all) are seldom if ever present. But three things are constant: books, her guitar, and her beloved sidekick, Larry. We get to meet this purple guy right away. As she did Chapter 5, Melanie lays out the storytime itinerary (what she does, how she does it, when she does it . . . and *why*). Sometimes, preschools bring their kids on visits to the library. Melanie conducts these storytimes just as she does the ones to an actual preschool.

The description of her women's shelter visits shows great sensitivity for some aspects of storytime that you may not have considered. The circumstances are so different from a library setting. The children (*and parents*) in your audience are often dealing with incredible emotional, physical, and personal stress. Book selection is delicate. Melanie has found that what worked best were not the popular books at all; they were the silly, fantastical books that made the kids laugh.

Recreation Center outreach comes naturally to a public library that collaborates with a city or county rec center. Often occurring just in the summer, and *outdoors*, these events are wide-ranging and involve lots of planning and organization. Packing a microphone and ensuring that there will be electricity are just two crucial components. Melanie shares a list of books for such events that are proven crowd-pleasers.

If you've ever been asked "Do you do birthday parties?" you will find what Melanie has to share on this topic of great interest. She's had some amusing adventures. A bear hunt ended up involving an entire house. Even the refreshments at one party were totally literacy based: gummy worms to accompany the reading of Eric Carle's *The Very Hungry Caterpillar.* Not to mention colored goldfish crackers for (have you guessed it?): *One Fish Two Fish Red Fish Blue Fish* by Dr. Seuss.

Melanie cried in Chapter 4. Readers may shed a tear over how she closes Chapter 6 with a moving account of what she has learned from her outreach experiences. *Now* may be the time to bring out that hankie!

AND . . . *now* may be time to finally turn to the chapter that has already sparked your interest. In the following pages, you'll probably discover things you're already doing, things you want to try as soon as your next storytime, and things you'll definitely do in the future, *and beyond.*

*Have fun!*

# Chapter 1

# All I Really Need to Know I Learned from ABC Books

Alphabet books are an incredible treasure trove that appeal to and can be used with almost any age. They're fun to look at, inspire questions (let's hear it for talking skills), can be found on a wide variety of topics, and enhance literacy.

This is the first ABC Book I ever had—*The Jolly Jump-Ups ABC Book* by Geraldine Clyne, published in 1948. It's still in great shape, considering that it's a pop-up book. Copies can be found on eBay, but I'm hanging onto mine. It's a hit with audiences.

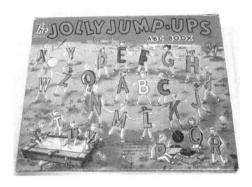

A big stack of regular ABC books accompanied me to every literacy workshop. I pointed them out at the end of my presentation as something extra that could add fun in a variety of ways and then let folks browse them. They always stimulated conversations among attendees.

I've often been asked to recommend a great alphabet book. I usually replied that there are so many terrific ones it would be hard to pick just one. Especially since there are those that concentrate on a particular topic—insects, space, animals, robots, penguins, firefighters, cowboys, monsters, ogres, dinosaurs, trains, ballet, butterflies, pirates, princesses, hats, superheroes, cats, dogs, pigs, bunnies, and so on. Early in my children's librarianship career when I was working with kids and books full-time, I began a personal list of ABC books. I made notes on each one I came across, starting with a few that I pulled for a specific storytime, those I noticed while working in the circulation area checking in returned books, plus some I spotted on the bookshelves while looking for something else. Alas, that list disappeared over the years.

Instead of feeling sad about the missing list, I took advantage of this opportunity to do new research on what ABC books are available today. I started with my own public library and was delighted to find many books I remembered using, plus loads of new titles. I had a chance to visit my daughter, a 2nd-grade teacher in Illinois, over her spring break, and she was happy to share a bin of ABC books that she keeps in her classroom. Her accumulation is composed of books she has found at thrift stores and garage sales. The librarian at her school found out what we were doing and asked to get involved. She pulled ABC books from her collection for me to look at while school was out. The school library's holdings included some recent books, but also old favorites, and even some *really* old favorites that had escaped being weeded when the school moved out of its 100-year-old building to a brand-new facility 3 years ago. In all, I looked at more than 250 ABC books for my research.

I didn't visualize this chapter as a list, so I've forced myself not to try to mention all 250. But I did want to highlight those that I know would be particularly useful in storytimes or other settings. Additionally, as I read more books I came up with activities that could be adapted in many ways. I wanted to describe some specific books along with examples of how each could reinforce the letters of the alphabet but also lead into something beyond. I briefly considered the term "mini-lesson" but discarded that immediately because it implies *work*. Learning will definitely be going on, but it will be done with stealth. So I opted for the term "ABC Mini-Adventure" to spark curiosity.

When thinking about literacy, I've always felt it's crucial to consider older youngsters and adults who have struggled with reading. These folks would no doubt be offended by "baby" or "kiddie" alphabet books, which can generally be found in profusion in most libraries. But lots of ABC books aren't designed for babies or kids anyway. Many of those were the inspiration for my Mini-Adventures. For example, consider *The Skull Alphabet Book* by Jerry Pallotta. The very first sentence is, "This is a science book about mammal skulls." Ralph Masiello's illustrations are amazing, and for some non-alphabet-related reason there are small portraits of all the U.S. presidents from George Washington through George W. Bush hidden in the drawings. So many fun components between two covers: skulls, words, colorful illustrations, and hidden objects! Are these few details about just one title enough to make you rush out and look for an armload of ABC books? How about the fact that this particular one is nonfiction and the colorful pictures require close examination (and re-examination)? That leads to repeat readings, not to mention great discussions! It's a win-win-win-win!

Trying to organize my notes into a coherent and intriguing narrative presented a problem, until I came up with the idea of putting them in ABC order! I've often thought it would be fun to write my own ABC book, and this may be the closest I'll ever get to that dream. So, I have included some very personal categories such as K is for Strikeout and U is for Underpants. Question: if you (or a youngster) were to create your own ABC book, what would you include?

This photo shows the back of a vest I wore whenever I did an early literacy workshop or presentation. It featured the library logo in sequins, my favorite art medium (after glitter, of course, which would have been impractical on a garment I wore often). Maybe wearing this vest on so many occasions somehow contributed to my preoccupation with ABC books . . . perhaps by osmosis?

The books I refer to in this chapter are based on personal whim and are ones I especially love. I felt truly liberated when I realized that I didn't have to include all 250+ books I reviewed for this chapter. I had fun looking at all of them and finding special surprises, such as familiar characters turning up unexpectedly. (I lost track of how often Ben Franklin appeared.) But I am excited to think that others will find gems and/or recurring items or characters of their own as they venture down new literacy paths using ABC books as landmarks. My favorite surprise was finding Elvis in three books!

Just as we have described sample storytimes elsewhere in this book, the books discussed in this chapter are sample "ABC Mini-Adventures" to help launch your own exploration of the infinite galaxy of alphabet books.

Although it raises a problem for me as a librarian, I'm placing **Q is for Quilt** at the top of the list. This was the first Mini-Adventure I came up with, and it has the most activities. I figure describing how this one evolved will demonstrate a framework that can be adapted for any subject.

# Q is for Quilt

There are several alphabet books based on quilts. Just one of these would be so great for a caregiver to read with a child and then talk about a family member who is/was a quilter. Maybe there is a well-loved quilt in the home that has an interesting history. A trip to a fabric or craft store would reinforce some illustrations from the book. Activities on this topic could be tailored depending on the age level of the child. A not-too-subtle lesson could be that letters go together to form words, just as a quilt is pieced together. Check Pinterest or Google under "quilt alphabet" for an array of examples that can be shared in many ways. Here are a few quilt-related books that could become a Quilt Mini-Adventure.

- *Sleepy ABC* by Margaret Wise Brown, pictures by Esphyr Slobodkina (HarperCollins 1953). Each letter relates to a bedtime scene in a quilt-like illustration. Simple rhymes are included.
- *Sleepy ABC* by Margaret Wise Brown, pictures by Karen Katz (HarperFestival 2016). This board book features Brown's words with new illustrations.
- *Quilt Alphabet* by Lesa Cline-Ransome, illustrated by James E. Ransome (Holiday House 2001). Each letter appears on a quilt block—great samples to re-create with cut paper or other art styles.
- *Eight Hands Round—A Patchwork Alphabet* by Ann Whitford Paul, illustrated by Jeanette Winter (HarperCollins 1991). Early patchwork quilt designs correspond to the letters of the alphabet, along with the patterns' derivations/histories.
- Although not an alphabet book, *The Log Cabin Quilt* by Ellen Howard, illustrated by Ronald Himler (Holiday House 1996), adds enrichment to the concept of quilts in American history. We follow Elvirey and her family as they move into a log cabin, and Granny's bag of quilt pieces helps turn the cabin into a home.

As my repertoire of ABC books expanded beyond 250, I frequently came across other references to quilts when I reached the "Q" page. These experiences reinforced the letter and provided a chance to think about other encounters with quilts in previous books. Imagine doing this with a child. What a great chance to talk about other "Q" words. Think of the fun suspense. Would there be a Quilt? Or would a Queen or a Quail be the chosen Q image? Would there be several Q words, including ones that *contained* Q, such as kumquat? I actually felt comforted when I ran across a quilt. There are plenty of children's books about quilts that could be added to this adventure, again depending on age level. But be sure to start off with at least one ABC book devoted to quilts.

# A is for Art

I found an Abundance of ABC books featuring Acclaimed Artists, which would Appeal to Artists of All Ages, As well As Art Aficionados.

- *I Spy: An Alphabet in Art*, devised and selected by Lucy Micklethwait (HarperCollins [United Kingdom]; Greenwillow Books [United States] 1992). Objects for each letter are highlighted from paintings by great artists. These aren't all easy to decode, although the picture entitled "Umbrellas" by Pierre Auguste Renoir is perfect for the letter U. Caution: there is some Picasso-style partial nudity on the art representing F, "Sitting Woman with a Fish Hat." A key is provided at the back of the book.
- *A Is for Artist: A Getty Museum Alphabet* by John Harris (published by the J. Paul Getty Museum, Los Angeles 1997). Small details from paintings are enlarged to feature a specific item: Candle for C, Pearl for P, Mustache for M. A picture gallery at the back of the book shows very small versions of all 26 masterpieces, and someone with sharp eyes should be able to spot the items featured earlier on the letter pages. Since there are works by the masters, there is nudity in some of the paintings, although none is shown in the vignettes on the letter pages.
- *M Is for Masterpiece: An Art Alphabet* by David Domeniconi, illustrated by Will Bullas (Sleeping Bear Press 2006). While introducing readers to famous artists, media, tools, and techniques, this A-Z pictorial uses not only simple poetry to introduce topics, but it also includes detailed expository text. Each featured artist is depicted with examples of their most famous works—other letters represent art objects or art forms.

# B is for Beasts

Lions and tigers and bears (not to mention katydids and unicorns and xeruses), oh my!

- *Tails, Claws, Fangs & Paws: An AlphaBeast Caper* by Terry Small (Bantam Books 1990). Reminiscent of *Animalia* (see **R Is for Read It Again and Again!**) with plenty of fun stuff to find, this book is not quite so jam-packed. An illustration key in the back tells what each animal in an illustration is, and there is also a glossary. A Weasel and a Woodchuck Wrestle a Wishbone; an Ibis does Ironing by an Igloo.
- *8: An Animal Alphabet* by Elisha Cooper (Orchard Books 2015). Would you believe there are 184 different animals featured in this book? For each letter of the alphabet there is at least one animal that starts with that letter (even Xerus for X), and for each

letter one animal is pictured eight times. For example, there are eight Koalas on the K page, along with a Kangaroo, a Kiwi, and other K animals. But the eight Xeruses are in a group all by themselves. Perhaps they're eXclusive!

- *ABC Animals* by the American Museum of Natural History (Sterling Children's Books 2013). In this book, we find a color photograph of each animal with the appropriate letter and a one- or two-sentence description. A Katydid climbs the K, a Sloth hangs from the upper loop of the S, and a Dolphin gracefully glides through the D. This book is an outstanding example of how letters and illustrations combine to inspire conversation and creativity.
- *V for Vanishing: An Alphabet of Endangered Animals* by Patricia Mullins, illustrations by Patricia Vaughan (HarperCollins Publishers 1993). Tissue paper collages illustrate endangered and even extinct animals. Particularly striking is the X spread, for Extinct, which depicts 10 animals that are no longer with us.
- *Zooflakes ABC* by Will C. Howell (Walker Publishing Company, Inc. 2002). An animal for each letter of the alphabet is represented by a snowflake cutout. Q = Quail, O = Octopus. Instructions and patterns are included. Since dexterity with sharp scissors is required, this would be a great ongoing project for an older youngster, making one snowflake every time you revisit the book.

# C is for Cats

Cats Conveniently Crop up in ABC books in Cahoots with the letter C, but there are Countless ABC books Consisting of felines.

- *A Is for Awful: A Grumpy Cat ABC Book* by Christy Webster, illustrated by Steph Laberis (A Little Golden Book, an imprint of Random House Children's Books, a division of Penguin Random House 2017). This would be perfect for someone in a bad mood who doesn't really want to read *any* ABC books! How can Grumpy Cat be grumpy with so many fun friends, including Iguana and Hedgehog?
- *K Is for Kitten* by Niki Clark Leopold, illustrated by Susan Jeffers (G. P. Putnam's Sons 2002). Lots of fun activities with a new kitten are depicted here, including yawns all around at the end of a busy day. Most charming illustration: K for Kitten compares the kitty's face to a pansy.
- I often used *Jeremy Kooloo* by Tim Mahurin (Dutton Children's Books, a division of Penguin Books, 1995) in storytimes. It was perfect when I was featuring cats, or in series of books about milk, and especially as a quick ABC book. This works for many age groups. Little kids will love that the story starts with ABC (A Big Cat) and is told letter by letter in order. Jeremy Kooloo Loves Milk, Nonfat (JKLMN). The full and sleepy kitty falls asleep under something that's very warm: a Quilt that features every letter of the alphabet, and appears alongside the list of all the words in the

story (which are in alphabetical order and manage to make sense!). It would be fun to make up a story using the alphabet as the framework.

# D is for Delicious

How often have we heard the phrases "Eat your vegetables!" and "Don't play with your food!"?

- *Healthy Foods from A to Z: Comida sana de la A à la Z*, edited by Stephanie Maze, photographs by Renée Comet (Moonstone Press 2012). This bilingual book will undoubtedly add new meaning to both of those admonitions. Fascinating faces made from fruits, vegetables, grains, dairy, and soy products stare out of the pages in surprise, sadness, joy, serenity, and plenty of other tasty emotions. Sometimes the words match the featured letter in both languages, sometimes not, but that just adds to the fun of learning new words (and foods!). Particularly delicious-looking are the ruby red pomegranate (*granada*) lips and the *pepino* (cucumber) ears on the P face. An extra letter appears on the N page: Ñ with tilde for *Ñame* (yam). Activities and projects are listed at the back along with descriptions of many of the foods used in the book and why they are good for us.

- *Eating the Alphabet—Fruits & Vegetables from A to Z* by Lois Ehlert (Harcourt 1989). Yes, apple shows up but so do some unfamiliar fruits and veggies. A parent commented to me that her kids loved this book because they were thinking about becoming vegetarians and this book contains such a wide variety of foods that they could eat (many of which they hadn't even heard of!).

- *An Alphabet Salad: Fruits and Vegetables from A to Z* by Sarah L. Schuette (Capstone Press 2003). Gorgeous photographs of a variety of edibles provide food for thought. In several illustrations, the featured item has been sliced open so that the insides are visible, such as F's Fig, K's Kiwifruit, and Q's Quince. Fruit and vegetable facts at the back tell us that a single yam can weigh as much as 100 pounds!

- *Mrs. Peanuckle's Fruit Alphabet* and *Mrs. Peanuckle's Vegetable Alphabet* are part of a recent ABC board book series (Rodale Kids 2017). These colorful books are truly fun and charming and contain fascinating food facts too. Can you name the only fruit whose seeds aren't inside? (Strawberry!) W is for Watermelon, and X is for Xigua— the Chinese and African name for watermelon. The illustrated fruits and veggies feature simple friendly faces, and some even sport mustaches!

- *A Is for Salad* by Mike Lester (Putnam & Grosset Group (a division of Penguin Putnam Books for Young Readers 2000). Despite the title, this really isn't a book about food. Each letter of the alphabet is presented in an unusual way. The meaning behind the title becomes clear when we see an alligator eating a bowl of greens. This might not make sense to a younger reader. However, an older child might enjoy looking at the funny illustrations and figuring out why a certain letter is used. My favorite: L is for hair dryer. A semi-disgusted-looking lion is shown blow-drying his mane.

# E is for Exploring

It's Easy to Encounter ABC books about specific Environments, locales, and areas, Either the city or state where you live, or someplace you've Envisioned visiting.

- I'm partial to *E Is for Enchantment: A New Mexico Alphabet* by Helen Foster James, illustrated by Neecy Twinem (Sleeping Bear Press 2004), just one of several state books by this author.
- *A Is for Aloha* by Stephanie Feeney, photographs by Hella Hammid (University Press of Hawaii 1980). This is an example of some extra fascinating tidbits you can discover by reading the author/illustrator notes or material usually included at the front or the back of the book. I found it interesting that over 35 years ago Ms. Feeney (author) wanted to produce a book that was relevant to the children of Hawaii and showed items that they were familiar with for each letter. But it is also an introduction to Hawaii for non-islanders. This book shows an example of the distinctive Hawaiian quilt style, a fun reminder of the **Q Is for Quilt** adventure. The children in nearly every black-and-white photo are from various Hawaiian preschools. You might not come across this specific book, but you might encounter something else just as engaging.
- Another black-and-white book is *Illinois from A to Z* by Betty Carlson Kay (University of Illinois Press 2000). Again, **Q Is for Quilt**, and there is information about the Illinois Quilt Research Project, which began documenting quilts in 1986.
- *Journey around Chicago from A to Z* by Martha Day Zschock (Commonwealth Editions 2005) is a super guidebook for someone coming to visit the Windy City. A bright red cardinal (state bird of Illinois) points out all the highlights and does cameo appearances as in the special rendition of Grant Wood's *American Gothic* painting in the Art Institute of Chicago. (This illustration is a reminder of the **A Is for Art** adventure.)

# F is for Feelings

When you Feel the *need*, the need to *read*!

- *A Is for Awesome* by Dallas Clayton (Candlewick Press 2014). This very kid-friendly book is a real confidence builder for someone who might feel insecure about their beginning reading efforts. The words for each letter are inspiring without talking down. For M the reader is encouraged to Make the Most of the day. R is for Radness, not to mention Reading. Each letter's main message is encircled by small drawings of relevant items (Queen, Quilt, Quarter, and Quail on Q), which all look like they might have been drawn and colored in by a child. This could easily inspire a reader to talk about or even illustrate his or her own favorite things that go with each letter.

- *F Is for Feelings* by Goldie Miller and Lisa A. Berger, illustrated by Hazel Mitchell (Free Spirit Publishing 2014). An extensive range of emotions are described in one or two sentences along with a colorful discussion-provoking illustration. A woman puts a bandage on a young boy's knee on the O page (O for Okay). N stands for Nervous as a girl deliberates about jumping into an older boy's arms in a pool, even though she has floaties on. The youngsters and adults depicted are diverse.

- I came across one ABC book that I would recommend for older teens and adults. It's called *What I Hate from A to Z* (Bloomsbury 2011), and the author/illustrator is *New Yorker* cartoonist Roz Chast. Her references to classic books, where she blames her fear of appendicitis on the book *Madeline* and *To Kill a Mockingbird* for her rabies aversion, made perfect sense to me. As did the slightly unnerving yet totally comprehensible cover illustration: a boy offering a yellow balloon to the familiar character in Edvard Munch's painting, *The Scream.* (Spoiler alerts: The book's appendix is a drawing showing the location of that exact organ, and the thing that Chast hates that starts with Y is *yellow*. Can you guess what she hates that starts with B?)

- If the previous book sounded appealing, you'll be thrilled to know that Roz Chast is the illustrator of *The Alphabet from A to Y with Bonus Letter Z!* by Steve Martin (Flying Dolphin Press 2007). Chast's drawings invite scrutiny, and you can almost hear Steve Martin reciting the alliterative rhymes for each letter. Extra extra bonus: Elvis sighting!

# G is for Gardening

Are you starting to dig ABC books? Wake up and smell the Gardenias! Gather your Gardening Gloves and Gadgets and Get Going!

- *A Garden Alphabet* by Isabel Wilner with pictures by Ashley Wolff (Dutton Children's Books 1991). The gardener in this story is a border collie whose helper is a frog. Rabbits, snails, mice, and grasshoppers are not welcome!

- *A Cottage Garden Alphabet* by Andrea Wisnewski (David R. Godine, Publisher 2002). Don't miss the attractive illustration of alphabet letters at the front of this book—all in black and white except for the A and the W which are red. (See if the reader can guess why these two letters are like this.) F is for Foxglove, and there's a little Fox peeking through the Fence and Ferns. (There are several F words in this illustration. Not every letter has more than one.) Illustrations inside are in color in the style of woodcuts, but the author explains in her note that they are really cut paper.

- *A Flower Fairy Alphabet* by Cicely Mary Barker (Published by the Penguin Group. Originally published in 1934, a new edition with new reproductions was published in 1990.) This small (4" × 6") volume is a jewel. A Flower Fairy is beautifully illustrated for almost all the letters in the alphabet, with an appropriate flower (F is for Fuchsia, Z for Zinnia). This isn't a must-have, but it's worth spending time on, just for the detailed illustrations and accompanying poems. Flower Fairies' fans will be thrilled to know there are seven other books in the series, including all four seasons.

# H is for Hands

Okay, I'll be Honest. I *do* have a favorite ABC book. It has a Home in my Heart.

- It's *The Handmade Alphabet* by Laura Rankin (Dial Books 1991). The manual alphabet, used in American Sign Language, is the basis of this book. Only the letter and a hand with the fingers shaped into the sign appear on a page. But there is no need for words. A hand in a blue Glove signs G. The hand in the sign for Q is resting on a Quilt. A Dragonfly is poised on the tip of the finger in the D sign. An X-ray of a hand making the sign for X is amazing. Each picture is done with colored pencil on charcoal paper. A wonderful show of hands—in a variety of ages and skin tones! I was happy to come across several sign language ABC books, and all of them feature folks of varying ages, ethnicities, and abilities.
- *Sign Language ABC* by Lora Heller (Sterling Children's Books 2012). Much like a basic ABC book with A is for Astronaut—great illustration, plus the sign language letter appears in a circle right under the letter.
- *My First Book of Sign Language* by Jan Holub (Scholastic 2001). Basic hand signs headline the pages, but additional signs for relevant things or activities are also included. The sign for ice cream is cool. Other helpful signs are included at the back of the book.
- *Handsigns: A Sign Language Alphabet* by Kathleen Fain (Chronicle Books 1993). Summary from book: Each letter and hand sign features a colorfully illustrated animal. They're not all predictable: V is for Vixen (female fox).

Speaking of hands, the Braille alphabet provides a great opportunity to learn and talk about how the blind learn to read. Although not ABC books, there are several titles on the topic.

- *Six Dots: A Story of Young Louis Braille* by Jen Bryant, illustrations by Boris Kulikov (Alfred A. Knopf 2016). I love the illustration of how Louis's sisters and father made letters for him out of straw, leather strips, and boards with round-topped nails pounded into letter shapes. This would be a fun activity to re-create, plus being a chance to explore the similarity between six-dot dominoes and the Braille alphabet.
- *A Black Book of Colors* by Menena Cottin and Rosana Faría, translated by Elisa Amado (Groundwood Books/House of Anansi Press 2008). Featured here are an embossed Braille alphabet and Braille versions of the text that accompanies the illustrations that are embossed on the facing pages. Many of these books have examples of Braille embossed in them, providing tactile examples. It's fun to feel strawberries for the description of red, feathers for yellow, and leaves for brown.

Further discussion could lead to a field trip to someplace with an elevator such as a hotel or hospital, where Braille is provided on the control panel, room signs, and so on.

# I is for Interests

Are you or your child Involved in a special Interest? As I mentioned in the Introductory matter to this chapter, there seems to be Infinity ABC book topics.

- Someone interested in the circus would find more than three rings of fun in *Who Put the B in the Ballyhoo? The Most Amazing, Bizarre, and Celebrated Circus Performers* by Carlyn Beccia (Houghton Mifflin 2007). But even the casual reader would enjoy learning how the word Jumbo came to mean big. (Note: it's not under E for Elephant but under X for eXtra large). There are details about circus performers from the past, and the illustrations are packed with delightful details. H stands for Hairy, and we learn about Annie Jones, an elegant bearded lady in the circus at the end of the 19th century. (Note the ABC in the subtitle: *Amazing, Bizarre, Celebrated*.)
- *ABC Is for Circus* by Patrick Hryby (AMMO Books 2010) is a much simpler book with just one word for each letter (J is for Juggler). The wildly colorful geometric illustrations make the pages pop and remind me of the artist Charley Harper. Amazing Art!

# J is for Juravenator

Since I Just mentioned Juggler in the previous adventure, I Jumped to the dictionary to find a different word to Justify J.

- Juravenator was a small (2-ft. long, 3.3 lbs.) carnivorous dinosaur that lived in the Jurassic Period. This is just one of the fun and fascinating dino details in the *Dinosaur Dictionary for Kids: The Everything Guide for Kids Who Love Dinosaurs* by Bob Korpella (Prufrock Press 2016). Publication data identifies an audience of grades 4–6, but I think younger and older readers would love this. With one exception, there is at least one dinosaur for every letter of the alphabet, so the first thing someone might do would be to find a dinosaur whose name matches their initial. Except for William or Wendy. But they're in luck, because they can use the "Create Your Own Dinosaur" page to make up their own Willisaurus or Wendanodon and choose its characteristics: carnivore or herbivore, feathered, armored, or scaly, length of tail, shape of tracks, and so on.
- There are plenty of dinosaur ABC books that cater to kids' preoccupation with dinos. Here's one that's a triple whammy of fun for dinosaur fans, truck fans, and puzzle fans: *Bang! Boom! Roar! A Busy Crew of Dinosaurs* by Nate Evans and Stephanie Gwyn Brown, illustrated by Christopher Santoro (HarperCollins Children's Books 2012). Twenty-three different kinds of dinosaurs appear throughout the book (they're

identified on the end papers at the front of the book). And almost that many types of trucks and big construction equipment are on the end papers at the back. The action-packed illustrations contain actual photographs of items such as tools and various foods, in the style of the *I Spy* Riddle books. There is even a list of hidden objects on the back cover. In addition to those, can you find a chocolate donut, a liver sandwich, and some pickles?

# K is for Strikeout

There's no crying in baseball, although batters might shed a few tears when they see a K next to their name in the box score. Don't believe me? Kindly consult the scorekeeper.

- The meaning of K is just one of the fun facts about America's pastime that you will learn in *ABCs of Baseball* by Peter Golenbock with pictures by Dan Andreasen (Dial Books for Young Readers, a division of Penguin Young Readers Group 2012). You'll be wanting to take this book and all the fans young and old that you know out to the ballpark. C doesn't just stand for Cracker Jack. See if you can stump your favorite baseball whiz with the question: What does "Can of Corn" refer to? (It's an easy-to-catch fly ball!)

There are lots more ABC books about baseball, but here are a few that hit it over the fence:

- *For the Love of Baseball: An A-to-Z Primer for Baseball Fans of All Ages* by Frederick C. Klein, illustrated by Mark Anderson (Triumph Books 2004). This is about famous players but includes lots of incidental factoids.
- *For the Love of the Cubs: An A-to-Z Primer for Cubs Fans of All Ages* by Frederick C. Klein, illustrated by Mark Anderson (Triumph Books 2003). Babe Ruth is mentioned even though he wasn't a Cub. Q stands for Queue—the line fans stand in to buy tickets or enter the stadium.
- *H Is for Home Run: A Baseball Alphabet* by Brad Herzog, illustrated by Melanie Rose (Sleeping Bear Press 2004). Babe Ruth turns up yet again.

# L is for Language

Enlarge the Love of Letters by sampling a new Language (or three!).

- *Marimba! Animales from A to Z* by Pat Mora, illustrations by Doug Cushman (Clarion Books, a division of Houghton Mifflin 2006). Who can resist the urge to join a parade of animals as they tango, salsa, cha cha, mambo, and conga through the zoo at night while their keepers are asleep? Author Mora has purposely included cognates (words that are similar in both English and Spanish), so readers may be surprised to realize they already know some words in another language. Between the rhyming and the dancing and the yummy foods that are mentioned, you might have to take a fiesta break halfway through this book and a siesta at the end. A pronunciation and translation guide to Spanish words that appear throughout the text is included.

- *Alphabet Times Four: An International ABC: English, Spanish, French, German* by Ruth Brown (Dutton Children's Books, a division of Penguin Books USA 1991). This is a book that deserves return visits. It's interesting that many things are spelled the same in all four languages, such as hamster, jaguar, kiwi, and yeti. Although they look the same, they sound different, as shown by the pronunciation guides given under each word. They would be identical, except that all nouns are capitalized in German. Some words are not at all similar: snake, *serpiente*, *serpent*, and *Schlange*. The illustrations stand up to close inspection. For example, the chameleon is hard to spot since he blends perfectly with his hiding place. And the X-ray of hands playing a xylophone is both spooky and compelling.

# M is for Mystery

Be Mystified by the Meeting of the Minds in this ABC adventure for fans of word play, puns, sight gags, searches, and challenges. To quote a famous sleuth, "The game's afoot!

- *Tomorrow's Alphabet* by George Shannon with pictures by Donald Crews (Greenwillow Books 1996). Once readers catch on to the "mystery" of this book they won't be able to stop. Something becomes something else, *tomorrow*. What might at first sound completely wrong, N is for twigs, for example, makes sense *tomorrow* when it becomes a Nest. Although sheep doesn't start with Y, it's tomorrow's Yarn. Q is for scraps, when you realize they turn into tomorrow's Quilt. Kids could easily come up with their own tomorrow's alphabet, such as O is for eggs, tomorrow's Omelet. I predict that once the premise of this book is understood, a family will start making up their own examples of tomorrow's alphabet.
- *The Z Was Zapped* by Chris Van Allsburg (Walter Lorraine Books, Houghton Mifflin Company 1987). According to the subtitle, this book is a play in 26 acts. Hmmm . . . 26 is a mysterious number but a significant one for alphabet fans. There are 26 mysteries in this book, but luckily, they are quickly solved by simply turning the page. Set in a theater, each letter appears on a stage and is experiencing something unpleasant. For example, the letter P is being attacked by a very determined bird. What's going on, given that we know it will be something starting with P? On the next page, we discover the P was Pecked. Van Allsburg tells us that this play is being performed by the Caslon Players—a little research leads one to the Caslon family of typefaces designed by William Caslon (c. 1692–1766) in London. Another ABC Mini-Adventure could be to follow the path into the history of moveable type, typesetting, printing, typewriters, and ultimately computers that provide a multitude of fonts.

A first step on the path could be found in the extra info at the front or back of a book where the typestyles that have been used are often mentioned.

- *Midnight in the Cemetery—A Spooky Search-and-Find Alphabet Book* by Cheryl Harness Simon, illustrated by Robin Brickman (Simon and Schuster Books for Young Readers 1999). The collage illustrations alone are a perfect reason to pick up this book. The technique is described in "A Note from the Illustrator" on page 3. The mystery in this book involves two children searching a graveyard for buried treasure, and the reader's task is to find objects hidden in the illustrations. Thankfully, a list of these appears on the final two pages, with some extra challenges as well. This book may be too intense for small children but should have eerie appeal for older kids, teens, and adults.

# N is for Names

Naturally, the first letter of a child's Name is Normally their favorite letter, as Noted in another Nook of this book. Imagine an entire ABC book based on Nothing but Names.

- Make that a *pair* of books. Dave Horowitz has written and illustrated *Twenty-Six Princesses* and *Twenty-Six Pirates* (Penguin Young Readers Books, published by The Penguin Group, 2008 and 2013). In the first book, 26 princesses, named for each letter of the alphabet, go to a party at the prince's castle. A wide variety of frogs appear throughout—maybe a hint about finding a prince? In the companion book, 26 pirates demonstrate their particular—and sometimes silly—talents and skills. Pirate Quaid is not afraid. (Even when some scary tentacles reach out from the ocean and threaten him!) The author credits the 1983 edition of *The New American Dictionary of Baby Names* as his bibliography.
- *Ogres! Ogres! Ogres! A Feasting Frenzy from A to Z* by Nicholas Heller, pictures by Jos. A. Smith (Greenwillow Books 1999). Ogres are named in order from Abednego to Zuleika. Each enjoys a food from the *next* letter of the alphabet. Odelle uses an ax to split Olives so she can eat the Pimentos. This book is a tasty alternative to cute animals and predictable food choices. Art lovers and puzzle fans will be challenged to find versions of artworks by Jasper Johns, Picasso, Rembrandt, and Rodin (and others!) hidden among the ogres in the basement.

# O is for Outstanding

There should be no Objections to describing the following ABC books in superlatives. They're brilliant, magnificent, superb, sensational, and wonderful. Or, as Charlotte might say: radiant, terrific . . . *some books*!

- *Turtle Island ABC* by Gerald Hausman, illustrated by Cara and Barry Moser (HarperCollins Publishers 1994). According to the author, Turtle Island is a Native

American name for North America. Pastel illustrations show soft-as-velvet images of symbols of the culture of The People (Native Americans). What we have here is an excellent example of an ABC book that could be studied by an older youngster or adult as much for the artistic technique as the word content. The various text passages are poetic by themselves. Hummingbird's description of mixing medicine with dewdrops in acorn shells evokes his role as the medicine man. While each illustration is predominantly monochromatic, taken all together the pages form a rainbow. Ears of corn, known as First Food, seem to float up from the page.

- *Alphabet under Construction* by Denise Fleming (Henry Holt and Company 2002). Speaking of artistic technique, the vivid illustrations in this book merit close examination because of the medium that Fleming employs: she creates handmade paper by pouring colored cotton fiber through hand-cut stencils. This sounds complicated, but the results are amazing. A young reader would find the depictions of a clever mouse constructing each letter exciting and fun. Older readers and adults might decide to experiment with Fleming's techniques themselves. She provides step-by-step instructions on her website: www .denisefleming.com. In fact, many authors and illustrators have personal websites that feature all kinds of information and activities to expand readers' enjoyment of their work. If you come across an author or illustrator whose works you admire, I recommend searching for their websites. You and your children will learn about these creative people and find enrichment activities, coloring sheets, puzzles, discussion guides, games, descriptions of their techniques, FAQs, and other resources. As I have mentioned before, interesting illustrations might be just the hook to land a reluctant reader of any age. Becoming fascinated by an illustrator's style could easily lead a reader to search out other books featuring their work, taking further steps along their path to literacy. What a fun way to become a fan (and a better reader)!

- *ABC: The Alphabet from the Sky* by Benedikt Groß/Gross and Joey Lee Price (Stern Sloan, an Imprint of Penguin Random House 2016). Have you ever looked out the window of a plane shortly after take-off or during descent and spotted letter shapes almost hidden in the landscape among roads, fields, neighborhoods, or buildings? This book is for you! Double-page spreads of aerial views contain lots to see, not just a specific letter shape hidden in plain (or is that plane?) sight. Longitude and latitude coordinates are provided for each location along with a miniature map of the United States that pinpoints the locale. A key in the back shows close-ups of the letters, and there are two more pages of letter shapes just for fun. Note: The author's name is often spelled Gross instead of Groß in library catalogs and on the Internet. The letter ß is part of the German alphabet and is the only letter not part of the Latin or Roman alphabet. Here's an opportunity to discuss and explore other alphabets: Cyrillic, Greek, Hebrew, and even Braille!

- While the previous book provides bird's eye or even satellite views as sources for letter shapes, *The Butterfly Alphabet* by Kjell B. Sandved (Scholastic 1996) highlights letter shapes found in the wings of butterflies. A rhyming couplet and a life-size picture of a butterfly appear opposite an extreme close-up of the butterfly's wing showing the shape of a letter in the scales. Fascinating info about butterflies in general and specific details on all the butterflies in the book are provided.

# P is for Picnic

Perhaps the next time you Pack your Picnic basket, you'll Put in an ABC book or two.

- *Pignic: An Alphabet Book in Rhyme* by Anne Miranda, illustrated by Rosekrans Hoffman (Boyds Mills Press 1996). Let's go to a swine family reunion with each member bringing a favorite food to share at the annual picnic. A fun feature is that each pig's name corresponds to a letter of the alphabet along with his dish: Ben's Boston Beans, Fern's Fifty Fried Fish, Violet's Vermicelli, and so on. Preceding foods appear again on subsequent pages, much like a familiar phrase often reappears in a story. It's fun to find characters from previous spreads turning up frequently. A pair of cats also grace some of the pages, providing the opportunity to chat about why they're there. A picture of two pigs seemingly communicating with one another via cell phone seems impossible in this nearly 20-year-old book. Can you guess what they're using? (It starts with W, and rhymes!)
- *Click, Clack, Quackity-Quack: An Alphabetical Adventure* by Doreen Cronin and Betsy Lewin (Atheneum Books for Young Readers 2005). Here's a fun chance to renew our friendship with the endearing animals we first met in *Click Clack Moo: Cows That Type* as they gather for a picnic. The cows' typewriter makes an early morning appearance—giving an opportunity to talk about this amazing machine and perhaps later look at a typewriter with a youngster and give them a chance to do some click-clacking of their own!

# Q is for Quilt

(If you're on a Quest for Q, Quickly look at the beginning of the list!)

# R is for Read It Again and Again!

Some ABC books are so Rich with illustrations that they Reinforce Re-viewing just to Recognize details that might have been missed on the first Reading.

- Who can resist returning to *I Spy A to Z—A Book of Picture Riddles* with riddles by Jean Marzollo and photographs by Walter Wick (Scholastic 2007)? This book and others by the same author and photographer provide hours of fun, hunting for various items described in the accompanying rhyming text. Readers might want to assemble their own picture riddles using personal items. It's fun to try and spy magnetic alphabet letters hiding on several pages.

- Don't miss *Animalia* by Graeme Base (25th anniversary edition published in 2012). Over 3 million copies of this book have been sold around the world. It's a must-see. It's like an *I Spy* riddle book except for a more sophisticated crowd. There is so much to discover in every spread. Base has even hidden some small drawings of himself in many of the pictures. (Hint: he has adapted the fashion statement first displayed by Waldo. Both wear striped shirts!) All the drawings are intricate, and it's hard to pick a favorite. But the P for Peacocks double-page spread might have the most items Pound for Pound, including a Peg-leg Pirate (with an eye Patch and a Parrot) carrying a Peace sign with the Pope.

# S is for Space

Do you know Someone with Stars in their eyes who's over the moon about outer Space?

- *Astronaut to Zodiac: A Young Stargazer's Alphabet* by Roger Ressmeyer (Crown Publishers 1992). You'll space out over the color photos in this book. Here's a fun fact from the letter X: the sun gives off X-rays in addition to light and heat. A glossary is included.
- *Stargazer's Alphabet* by John Farrell (Boyds Mills Press 2007). Combine this book with a visit to a planetarium or a night-time telescopic sky scan to spot constellations. It's a painless way to learn about stars and coincidentally pick up a lot of mythology. A pronunciation key helps with words like Andromeda and Io.
- *Touchdown Mars* by Peggy Wethered and Ken Edgett, illustrated by Michael Chesworth (G. P. Putnam's Sons 1999). Our crew is comprised of a diverse cast of youngsters and characters and includes a cat with its own rainbow-striped space suit. It begins with Astronaut and goes to Zero, the last number in a countdown. Packed with details about a trip to Mars, an A-B-Cyclopedia at the end provides further facts about the red planet.

# T is for Trucks

Transportation and Traffic Too! Terrific!

- *Alphabet Trucks* by Samantha R. Vamos, illustrated by Ryan O'Rourke (Charlesbridge 2013). Who knew there were so many kinds of trucks! It would be fun to read about all of them and then try spotting some on the road, near a harbor, or at a fire station. In this book, Q stands for Quint (short for Quintuple) truck—a super fire engine that has several kinds of firefighting apparatus including ladders, pumps, booster tanks, and hoses. In the illustration for this truck, the letter Q is being rescued from a tree, while the R (for Recycling) truck is going down the opposite side of the street. Double-page spreads at the front and back show all the trucks with their corresponding letters. Trying to name all the different kinds of trucks would be a fun game. This would take more than one reading, but I'm sure a youngster who loves trucks would learn them all quickly.

- *Race from A to Z* by Jon Scieszka, illustrated by Dani Jones (Simon & Schuster Books for Young Readers 2014). A variety trucks race through the streets of Trucktown. Izzy the Ice cream truck plays a crucial role throughout.

- *ABCs on Wheels* by Ramon Olivera (Little Simon, an imprint of Simon & Schuster Books for Young Readers 2016). Technically, this book isn't just trucks; it includes the moon Rover for R. The Limousine for L takes up almost an entire double-page spread (surrounded by a Motorcade for M). It's fun to see that once again an Ice cream truck gets the scoop on I.

# U is for Underpants

Understandably, it might seem Unusual that Underwear is just about Universally Ubiquitous in ABC books, Unless you Uncover Unicorns and Umbrellas.

- *SuperHero ABC* by Bob McLeod (HarperCollins Children's Books 2006). Author/illustrator McLeod has a comic book background, but the heroes in this book are all his own creations. This diverse bunch will no doubt inspire youngsters to dream up their own heroes. Upside-Down Man wears his Uniform under his Underwear (yep, tighty whiteys!). Ms. Incredible can become Instantly Invisible. There is a satisfying amount of grossness as well, including the Odor Officer and The Volcano (he Vomits on Villains), which will appeal to kids.

- *Peanut Butter and Jellyfishes: A Very Silly Alphabet Book* by Brian P. Cleary, illustrated by Betsy E. Snyder (Millbrook Press 2006). Another fun-packed book with lots to see on multiple viewings. The collage illustrations are so animated that they might inspire creativity. The rhymes are fun and contain a few of the words for each letter, plus additional items that aren't named appear. Many of these turn up in the end sheets which might lead to another reading immediately just to find them. Some friends from other books are back; a Quilt is shown on the Q page but not mentioned by name. Elvis shows up as a gardener on the E page, and the ever-popular Underpants appear on a clothesline spanning U. Don't miss the tiny mouse riding an even-tinier Unicycle.

- *What Pete Ate from A-Z (Really!)* by Maira Kalman (G. P. Putnam's Sons, a division of Penguin Putnam Books for Young Readers 2001). Fun from beginning to end, Kalman's quirky illustrations match the incredible variety of things that her dog, Pete, ate, starting with an Accordion. He refuses the Z, however, which stands for Zug Zug Dog Grub. Predictably, Pete even eats Cousin Rocky's Underpants, monogram, and all. The subtitle lets us know what we're in for: "Where we explore the English Alphabet (in its entirety) in which a certain Dog devours a myriad of items which he should not."

# V is for Vintage

Have you been surprised by something that you had almost forgotten about? That's a blast from the past.

- *Toys ABC: An Alphabet Book* by B. A. Hoena (Capstone Press 2005). Colorful photos show lots of toys a child might be familiar with and a few uncommon/vintage ones. Q is for a Queen from a chess set; U for Ukulele. There are plenty of opportunities for a discussion of what kinds of toys were popular with the parent or grandparent. Diverse people are shown.
- *A Is for Annabelle: A Doll's Alphabet* by Tasha Tudor (Oxford University Press 1954, later edition Simon & Schuster Books for Young Readers 2001). Annabelle is grandmother's doll, and two little girls are playing with her carefully, inspecting her clothes and belongings. Tudor's unmistakable style is showcased on every page. She was a Caldecott Honor winner but not for this book. Q is for Quilt, but there are some new words as well: cloak, kerchief, muff, nosegay, parasol, veil, and so on, which are excellent examples of using illustrations as context to learn the meaning of words. Grandmas of today sharing this with their grandchildren will no doubt be reminded of their own grandmothers.
- *A Apple Pie* by Kate Greenaway (Frederick Warne & Co. original woodblock designs engraved in 1856; 2012 edition by Watchmaker Publishing). Notes explain that the text is based on a rhyme from 1671; included is a history of the alphabet which at the time of original publication did not differentiate between the I and the J. Looking at the charming illustrations one can understand why the British Caldecott equivalent was named for Greenaway. (See **W Is for Winners** next.)

# W is for Winners

And the award goes to . . .

I came across a couple of ABC books that had won Caldecott Honors (runner-up to the Caldecott Medal) in 1996 and 1997. Since I've mentioned the art in ABC books several times, I was curious to find out if other ABC books had received these prestigious awards. There have been seven Caldecott Honor winners and one Caldecott Medal winner. Additionally, one book received a Newbery Honor designation in 1934, a few years before the separate category for artist/illustration was established. The Caldecott Medal, begun in 1937, was named in honor of 19th-century English illustrator Randolph Caldecott. It is awarded annually by the Association for Library Service to Children, a division of the American Library Association, to the artist of the most distinguished American picture book for children. The Newbery Medal, established in 1922, was named for 18th-century British bookseller John Newbery. It is awarded annually by the Association for Library Service to Children, a division of the American Library Association, to the author of the most distinguished contribution to American literature for children. I've listed the books at the end of this paragraph in chronological order of the year of their award. Publication dates are the previous year. I've included the name of the illustrator if it is different from the author. One book, *An American ABC* by the Petershams and published in 1941, may be hard to find. It has probably disappeared from most libraries due to wear and tear, not to mention outdated and controversial content (the flag had just 48 stars at the time of publication, and Native Americans are referred to by an R word that is objectionable even today). But the illustrations are the reason for the award, and many of them are stirringly patriotic in harmony with the time. I was fortunate to see a copy of the book in the de Grummond Children's Literature Collection at the University of Southern Mississippi, and am glad such books are preserved in archives like this. I'll leave it up to you to peruse the books and see if you think they are award-worthy. (Note: one book is wordless*, opening up endless discussion possibilities.)

- 1934—Newbery Honor—*The ABC Bunny* by Wanda Gág (originally published by Coward McCann, more recently by The Putnam Grosset Group)
- 1942—Caldecott Honor—*An American ABC* by Maud and Miska Petersham (Macmillan)
- 1953—Caldecott Honor—*Ape in a Cape: An Alphabet of Odd Animals* by Fritz Eichenberg (Houghton Mifflin Harcourt)
- 1973—Caldecott Honor—*Hosie's Alphabet* illustrated by Leonard Baskin, words by Hosea Tobias Baskin (Viking Press)
- 1975—Caldecott Honor—*Jambo Means Hello: A Swahili Alphabet Book* illustrated by Tom Feelings, words by Muriel Feelings (Dial Press)
- 1977—Caldecott Medal—*Ashanti to Zulu: African Traditions* illustrated by Leo & Diane Dillon, words by Margaret Musgrove (Dial Press)
- 1987—Caldecott Honor—*Alphabatics* by Suse MacDonald (Simon & Schuster Books for Young Readers)
- 1996—Caldecott Honor—**Alphabet City* by Stephen T. Johnson (Puffin Books)
- 1997—Caldecott Honor—*The Graphic Alphabet* by David Pelletier (Scholastic)

#  is for eXercise

Expand your mind, develop your reading muscles, and get in shape with ABC books.

- *The Turn-Around, Upside-Down Alphabet Book* by Lisa Campbell Ernst (Simon & Schuster Books for Young Readers 2004). This book encourages play as the reader rotates it in different directions. Each brightly colored large letter has a complimentary background. As you rotate the book, you see incredibly simple graphics that match the accompanying description. The N looks like a snake, then a tunnel, and then a couple of tortilla chips on their way to guacamole. Besides being good exercise by moving the book like a windmill, the letters could become an art project with each one being a game piece that players would manipulate to find something new.

- *Keeping Fit from A to Z/Mantente en forma de la A à la Z*, edited by Stephanie Maze (Moonstone Press 2014). This bilingual book is similar in style to another book by Maze, which I described in **D Is for Delicious**. More than 150 action-filled color photos showcase a diverse collection of children doing all kinds of sports, exercises, and fitness activities, as well as traditional games from a variety of cultures. English words appear in white, Spanish words in color on the busy pages. Additional activities and games are described at the end of the book along with facts for parents about the importance of exercise for children. Definitely not a bedtime read, this book will lead to movement motivation, jumping for joy, and hopping for happiness!

# Y is for Yucky

Yep! Young and old will Yell "Yahoo!" No Yawns in these books!

- *The Absolutely Awful Alphabet* by Mordicai Gerstein (Harcourt Brace & Company 1999). A great book for a youngster who is a reluctant reader but loves monsters and is perhaps inclined to draw such things. Many of the words require a trip to the dictionary (not a bad thing!), such as ignoramus or monstrosity. A good place to start would be with the readers' initials and a discussion of how they might illustrate it themselves. Valerie or Victor would no doubt delight in the Vampire V, a Voracious Vegetable.
- *The Yucky Reptile Alphabet Book* by Jerry Pallotta, illustrated by Ralph Masiello (Charlesbridge Publishing 1989). C is for Chameleon, whose tongue is so long that it appears on three pages of this book—almost twice as long as the chameleon's body. Speaking of length—some Boas (for B) can be as long as a school bus! N is for Night snake—a creature hard to see in a tree after dark! This is just one of several great ABC books by Pallotta.
- *The Furry Animal Alphabet Book* by Jerry Pallotta, illustrated by Edgar Stewart (Charlesbridge 1991). Fascinating fact: U is for Unau, a sloth with two toes on each foot. They don't move around much, and green mold has been known to grow on their fur. *Yucky*, yes?

# Z is for Zany

Caution: ABC books are Zesty. You may become Zealous about them. There is Zero chance that a kid won't be Zonked by them too. (Unless they're a Zombie!)

- *Z Is for Moose* by Kelly Bingham, pictures by Paul O. Zelinsky (Greenwillow Books, an imprint of HarperCollins Publishers 2012). This book starts out conventionally, A is for Apple, B is for Ball, and C is for Cat. But things turn zany when Moose tries to strong-arm his way into the ABC pageant being put together by Zebra. Big fun and lots of action.

- *LMNO Peas* by Keith Baker (Beach Lane Books, an imprint of Simon and Schuster Children's Publishing Division 2010). This title alone is sure to bring a smile to anyone (like *me*!) who still frequently whispers "L, M, N, O, P" when looking up words in the dictionary, or shopping for spices at the grocery store, or tracking down an author on a library's fiction shelves. The pod-dwellers in this book show off a variety of capital letters representing jobs, from Astronaut to Zoologist. I once read that Keith Baker likes to "hide" something on each page spread—in this book it's a tiny ladybug. Besides ladybugs, there are lots of fun things to find that might appeal to older kids or even adults. My favorite is the K page that shows two Kings. One wears a crown, the other one is singing into a microphone—he has a distinctive black hairdo complete with sideburns. *LMNO Pea-quel* (featuring lower-case letters) was published in 2017.

- *Alphabatty: Riddles from A to Z* by Rick and Ann Walton, pictures by Susan Slattery Burke (Lerner Publications Company 1991). Certain people love riddles, and they will delight in this book. The riddles are thought-provoking, yet not too hard to figure out. They should probably be taken in small doses of not more than three at a time, however, to avoid boring others and sending them to the land of Zzzzzzzzzzzz.

Have I sold you on ABC books yet? Just in case, here are a few more selling points:

- ☐ ABC books can be used for different ages. In many of the books, younger children will pick up new vocabulary in the simple verses. Older children can learn more details about each word from the longer descriptive material. Kids are smarter than we think and are often interested in much more sophisticated things than we might expect.

- ☐ Some ABC books that contain puzzles or things that are hidden include the answers at the back, and some that have secrets or surprises in the illustrations might not have such a thing on every page. *And some don't.* As always, it's a good idea to preview a book. In addition, establishing the fact that there might not always be something hidden can help avoid that dreaded F word—Frustration.

- ☐ Find as many ABC books as you can in your local library; others may be available inexpensively via secondary markets including eBay and Amazon.

- ☐ Be on the lookout for ABC books at garage sales, library used book sales, and thrift shops. My daughter is constantly picking these up to add to her classroom library and now has two big bins of ABC books—plenty to go around for a time in class when everyone picks out an ABC book to look at and share similarities and differences. ("Who's got a Quilt for Q?")

- ☐ Taking the previous example a little further, consider using ABC books in ESL (English as a Second Language) classes. Depending on class size, discussion could revolve around how words for certain things differ. Do they start with the same letter? Make lists of items that are similar in multiple languages.

- ☐ Search topics on Pinterest, Google, and Google Images: Alphabet, Alphabet Crafts, Letter Crafts, Alphabet Coloring Pages, Alphabet Activities, and more!

- ☐ Art teachers can probably think up an art project to go with just about any ABC book, based on the subject matter, the style/technique of the illustrations, font choices, and even the way type is displayed.

- [ ] One of the best ABC books is the dictionary! It's fun to find a word, learn the definition, see it used in a sentence, and discover the synonyms. There are lots of online dictionaries, but an actual printed copy is valuable too. Paperback editions are fine, and used copies are totally practical. Age-appropriate versions are good, but upper-level works help stretch the mind. Dictionaries make excellent gifts!
- [ ] Caution: If you give a kid a dictionary, you'll probably have to throw in a thesaurus too.
- [ ] Here's a wonderful word: *abecedarium*. It's from Medieval Latin and refers to a primer for teaching the alphabet. Since I'm nuts about ABC books, does that make me an *Abecedarian Librarian*?
- [ ] Seeking a cure for an ABC book addiction? How about a nice bowl of Alphabet Soup?

# REFERENCES

Note: Letter in **BOLD** following citation refers to the ABC Mini-Adventure in which it appears.

Baker, Keith. 2010. *LMNO Peas.* New York: Little Simon, an imprint of Simon & Schuster Children's Publishing Division. **Z**

Barker, Cicely Mary. 1934, 1990. *A Flower Fairy Alphabet.* London, Glasgow: Blackie & Son Limited. London: Frederick Warne. **G**

Base, Graeme. 2001. *Animalia 25th Anniversary Edition.* Melbourne: Viking. **R**

Baskin, Leonard, and Hosea Tobias Baskin. 1972. *Hosie's Alphabet.* New York: Viking Press. **W**

Beccia, Carlyn. 2007. *Who Put the B in the Ballyhoo? The Most Amazing, Bizarre, and Celebrated Circus Performers.* New York: Houghton Mifflin. **I**

Bingham, Kelly. 2012. *Z Is for Moose.* Paul O. Zelinsky, illustrator. New York: Greenwillow Books, an imprint of HarperCollins Publishers. **Z**

Brown, Margaret Wise. 1953. *Sleepy ABC.* Esphyr Slobodkina, illustrator. New York: HarperCollins. **Q**

Brown, Margaret Wise. 2016. *Sleepy ABC.* Karen Katz, illustrator. Board book. New York: HarperFestival. **Q**

Brown, Ruth. 1991. *Alphabet Times Four: An International ABC: English, Spanish, French, German.* New York: Dutton Children's Books. **L**

Bryant, Jen. 2016. *Six Dots: A Story of Young Louis Braille.* Boris Kulikov, illustrator. New York: Alfred A. Knopf. **H**

Chast, Liz. 2011. *What I Hate from A to Z.* New York: Bloomsbury. **F**

Clayton, Dallas. 2014. *A Is for Awesome.* Somerville, MA: Candlewick Press. **F**

Cleary, Brian P. 2006. *Peanut Butter and Jellyfishes: A Very Silly Alphabet Book.* Betsy E. Snyder, illustrator. New York: Millbrook Press.

Cline-Ransome, Lesa. 2001. *Quilt Alphabet.* James E. Ransome, illustrator. New York: Holiday House. **Q**

Clyne, Geraldine. 1948. *The Jolly Jump-Ups ABC Book.* Springfield, MA: McLoughlin Bros., Inc.

Cooper, Elisha. 2015. *8: An Animal Alphabet.* New York: Orchard Books. **B**

Cottin, Menena, and Rosana Faria. 2008. *A Black Book of Colors.* Elisa Amado, translator. Toronto: Groundwood Books/House of Anansi Press. **H**

Cronin, Doreen, and Betsy Lewin. 2005. *Click, Clack, Quackity-Quack: An Alphabetical Adventure.* New York: Atheneum Books for Young Readers. **P**

Domeniconi, David. 2006. *M Is for Masterpiece: An Art Alphabet.* Will Bullas, illustrator. Chelsea, MI: Sleeping Bear Press. **A**

Ehlert, Lois. 1989. *Eating the Alphabet—Fruits & Vegetables from A to Z.* New York: Harcourt. **D**

Eichenberg, Fritz. 1952. *Ape in a Cape: An Alphabet of Odd Animals.* New York: Houghton Mifflin Harcourt. 1952. **W**

Ernst, Lisa Campbell. 2004. *The Turn-Around, Upside-Down Alphabet Book.* New York: Simon & Schuster Books for Young Readers. **X**

Evans, Nate, and Stephanie Gwyn Brown. 2012. *Bang! Boom! Roar! A Busy Crew of Dinosaurs.* Christopher Santoro, illustrator. New York: HarperCollins Children's Books. **J**

Fain, Kathleen. 1993. *Handsigns: A Sign Language Alphabet.* San Francisco: Chronicle Books. **H**

Farrell, John. 2007. *Stargazer's Alphabet.* Honesdale, PA: Boyds Mills Press. **S**

Feelings, Muriel and Tom. 1974. *Jambo Means Hello: A Swahili Alphabet Book.* New York: Dial Press. **W**

Feeney, Stephanie. 1980. *A Is for Aloha.* Hella Hammid, photographer. Honolulu: University Press of Hawaii. **E**

Fleming, Denise. 2002. *Alphabet under Construction.* New York: Henry Holt and Company. **O**

Ford, Jessie. 2017. *Mrs. Peanuckle's Fruit Alphabet.* Emmaus, PA: Rodale Kids. **D**

Ford, Jessie. 2017. *Mrs. Peanuckle's Vegetable Alphabet.* Emmaus, PA: Rodale Kids. **D**

Gág, Wanda. 1933 & 1997. *The ABC Bunny.* New York: Coward McCann. New York: The Putnam & Grosset Group. **W**

Gerstein, Mordicai. 1999. *The Absolutely Awful Alphabet.* San Diego: Harcourt Brace & Company. **Y**

Golenbock, Peter. 2012. *ABCs of Baseball.* Dan Andreasen, illustrator. New York: Dial Books for Young Readers. **K**

Greenaway, Kate. 1856 & 2012. *A Apple Pie* London: Frederick Warne & Co. original woodblock designs engraved in 1856. Ocean Shores, WA: Watchmaker Publishing. **V**

Groß/Gross, Benedikt, and Joey Lee Price. 2016. *ABC: The Alphabet from the Sky.* New York: Stern Sloan. **O**

Harris, John. 1997. *A Is for Artist: A Getty Museum Alphabet.* Los Angeles: The J. Paul Getty Museum. **A**

Hausman, Gerald. 1994. *Turtle Island ABC.* Cara and Barry Moser, illustrators. New York: HarperCollins Publishers. **O**

Heller, Lora. 2012. *Sign Language ABC.* New York: Sterling Children's Books. **H**

Heller, Nicholas. 1999. *Ogres! Ogres! Ogres! A Feasting Frenzy from A to Z.* Jos. A. Smith, illustrator. New York: Greenwillow Books. **N**

Herzog, Brad. 2004. *H Is for Home Run: A Baseball Alphabet.* Melanie Rose, illustrator. Ann Arbor, MI: Sleeping Bear Press. **K**

Hoena, B. A. 2005. *Toys ABC: An Alphabet Book.* Mankato, MN: Capstone Press. **V**

Holub, Jan. 2001. *My First Book of Sign Language.* New York: Scholastic. **H**

Horowitz, Dave. 2008. *Twenty-Six Princesses.* New York: Penguin Young Readers Books, published by The Penguin Group. **N**

Horowitz, Dave. 2013. *Twenty-Six Pirates.* New York: Penguin Young Readers Books, published by The Penguin Group. **N**Howard, Ellen. 1996. *The Log Cabin Quilt.* Ronald Himler, illustrator. New York: Holiday House. **Q**

Howell, Will C. 2002. *Zooflakes ABC.* New York: Walker Publishing Company, Inc. **B**

Hryby, Patrick. 2010. *ABC Is for Circus.* Los Angeles: AMMO Books. **I**

James, Helen Foster. 2004. *E Is for Enchantment: A New Mexico Alphabet.* Neecy Twinem, illustrator. Ann Arbor, MI: Sleeping Bear Press. **E**

Johnson, Stephen T. 1995. *Alphabet City.* New York: Puffin Books. **W**

Kalman, Maira. 2001. *What Pete Ate from A-Z (Really!).* New York: G. P. Putnam's Sons, a division of Penguin Putnam Books for Young Readers. **U**

Kay, Betty Carlson. 2000. *Illinois from A to Z.* Urbana: University of Illinois Press. **E**

Klein, Frederick C. 2003. *For the Love of the Cubs: An A-to-Z Primer for Cubs Fans of All Ages.* Mark Anderson, illustrator. Chicago: Triumph Books. **K**

Klein, Frederick C. 2004. *For the Love of Baseball: An A-to-Z Primer for Baseball Fans of All Ages.* Mark Anderson, illustrator. Chicago: Triumph Books. **K**

Korpella, Bob. 2016. *Dinosaur Dictionary for Kids: The Everything Guide for Kids Who Love Dinosaurs.* Waco, TX: Prufrock Press. **J**

Leopold, Niki Clark. 2002. *K Is for Kitten.* Susan Jeffers, illustrator. New York: G. P. Putnam's Sons. **C**

Lester, Mike. 2000. *A Is for Salad.* New York: Putnam & Grosset Group, a division of Penguin Putnam Books for Young Readers. **D**

MacDonald, Suse. 1986. *Alphabatics.* New York: Simon & Schuster Books for Young Readers. **W**

Manhurin, Tim. 1995. *Jeremy Kooloo.* New York: Dutton Children's Books, a division of Penguin Books. **C**

Martin, Steve. 2007. *The Alphabet from A to Y with Bonus Letter Z!* Roz Chast, illustrator. New York: Flying Dolphin Press. **F**

Marzollo, Jean. 2007. *I Spy A to Z—A Book of Picture Riddles.* Walter Wick, photographer. New York: Scholastic. **R**

Maze, Stephanie, editor. 2012. *Healthy Foods from A to Z: Comida sana de la A à la Z.* Renée Comet, photographer. Sarasota, FL: Moonstone Press. **D**

Maze, Stephanie, editor. 2014. *Keeping Fit from A to Z/Mantente en forma de la A à la Z.* Sarasota, FL: Moonstone Press. **X**

McLeod, Bob. 2006. *SuperHero ABC.* New York: HarperCollins Children's Books. **U**

Micklethwait, Lucy. 1992. *I Spy: An Alphabet in Art.* London: Harper Collins (United Kingdom). New York: Mulberry Books (United States). **A**

Miller, Goldie, and Lisa A. Berger. 2014. *F Is for Feelings.* Hazel Mitchell, illustrator. Minneapolis: Free Spirit Publishing. **F**

Miranda, Anne. 1996. *Pignic: An Alphabet Book in Rhyme.* Rosekrans Hoffman, illustrator. Honesdale, PA: Boyds Mills Press. **P**

Mora, Pat. 2006. *Marimba! Animales from A to Z.* Doug Cushman, illustrator. New York: Clarion Books, a division of Houghton Mifflin. **L**

Mullins, Patricia. 1993. *V for Vanishing: An Alphabet of Endangered Animals.* Patricia Vaughan, illustrator. New York: HarperCollins Publishers. **B**

Musgrove, Margaret. 1976. *Ashanti to Zulu: African Traditions.* Leo and Diane Dillon, illustrators. New York: Dial Press. **W**

Olivera, Ramon. 2016. *ABCs on Wheels.* New York: Little Simon, an imprint of Simon & Schuster Books for Young Readers. **T**

Pallotta, Jerry. 1989. *The Yucky Reptile Alphabet Book.* Ralph Masiello, illustrator. Watertown, MA: Charlesbridge. 1989. **Y**

Pallotta, Jerry. 1991. *The Furry Animal Alphabet Book.* Edgar Stewart, illustrator. Watertown, MA: Charlesbridge. **Y**

Pallotta, Jerry. 2002: *The Skull Alphabet Book.* Ralph Masiello, illustrator. Watertown, MA: Charlesbridge.

Paul, Ann Whitford. 1991. *Eight Hands Round—A Patchwork Alphabet.* Jeanette Winter, illustrator. New York: HarperCollins. **Q**

Pelletier, David. 1996. *The Graphic Alphabet.* New York: Scholastic. **W**

Petersham, Maud, and Miska Petersham. 1941. *An American ABC.* New York: Macmillan. **W**

Rankin, Laura. 1991. *The Handmade Alphabet.* New York: Dial Books. **H**

Ressmeyer, Roger. 1992. *Astronaut to Zodiac: A Young Stargazer's Alphabet.* New York: Crown Publishers. **S**

Sandved, Kjell B. 1996. *The Butterfly Alphabet.* New York: Scholastic. **O**

Schuette, Sarah L. 2003. *An Alphabet Salad: Fruits and Vegetables from A to Z.* Mankato, MN: Capstone Press. **D**

Scieszka, Jon. 2014. *Race from A to Z.* Dani Jones, illustrator. New York: Simon & Schuster Books for Young Readers. **T**

Shannon, George. 1996. *Tomorrow's Alphabet.* Donald Crews, illustrator. New York: Greenwillow Books. **M**

Simon, Cheryl Harness. 1999. *Midnight in the Cemetery—A Spooky Search-and-Find Alphabet Book.* Robin Brickman, illustrator. New York: Simon and Schuster Books for Young Readers. **M**

Small, Terry. 1990. *Tails, Claws, Fangs & Paws: An AlphaBeast Caper.* New York: Bantam Books. **B**

Sterling Children's Books. 2013. *ABC Animals by the American Museum of Natural History.* New York: Sterling Children's Books. **B**

Tudor, Tasha. 1954 and 2001. *A Is for Annabelle: A Doll's Alphabet.* Oxford, UK: Oxford University Press. Later edition New York: Simon & Schuster Books for Young Readers. **V**

Vamos, Samantha R. 2013. *Alphabet Trucks.* Ryan O'Rourke, illustrator. Watertown, MA: Charlesbridge. **T**

Van Allsburg, Chris. 1987. *The Z Was Zapped.* Boston: Walter Lorraine Books, Houghton Mifflin Company. **M**

Walton, Rick, and Ann Walton. 1991. *Alphabatty: Riddles from A to Z.* Susan Slattery Burke, illustrator. Minneapolis: Lerner Publications Company. **Z**

Webster, Christy. 2017. *A Is for Awful: A Grumpy Cat ABC Book.* Steph Laberis, illustrator. New York: A Little Golden Book, an imprint of Random House Children's Books, a division of Penguin Random House. **C**

Wethered, Peggy, and Ken Edgett. 1999. *Touchdown Mars.* Michael Chesworth, illustrator. New York: G. P. Putnam's Sons. **S**

Wilner, Isabel. 1991. *A Garden Alphabet.* Ashley Wolff, illustrator. New York: Dutton Children's Books. **G**

Wisnewski, Andrea. 2002. *A Cottage Garden Alphabet.* Boston: David R. Godine, Publisher. **G**

Zschock, Martha Day. 2005. *Journey around Chicago from A to Z.* Beverly, MA: Commonwealth Editions. **E**

# Chapter 2

# Literacy Doodads: Not Just Letter Magnets on the Refrigerator Anymore!

Okay, I know what you're thinking: What's a Doodad? In general, *doodad* is a word used to refer to something when the actual name of it is unknown or forgotten. The plural *doodads* is a term for a group of items that have something in common but aren't alike. For example, a "doodads drawer" in the kitchen that holds a variety of items. So what are "literacy doodads"?

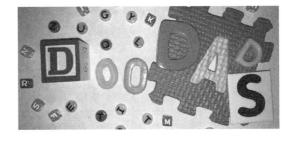

I would bet that every children's librarian has a drawer or a box or a bag containing an assortment of items related to the alphabet: ABC books, blocks, puzzles, stickers, toys, and more. They're all valuable when the topic of literacy comes up. But what's a succinct way to refer to them? Whenever I do an early literacy workshop or presentation I bring along my accumulation of what I call Literacy Doodads. I didn't consciously start out to collect these things. I just came across alphabet items that fascinated me, and I figured they would probably fascinate kids too. And the collection is still growing!

Are you a parent, grandparent, caregiver, and/or librarian looking for tips to enhance early literacy? You may find a few ideas based on the doodads in this chapter to make your reading interactions memorable, enjoyable, and fun for all.

There are a lot of early literacy programs used by libraries, including Every Child Ready to Read (ECRR; American Library Association), 6 by 6, Mother Goose on the Loose, the Very Ready Reading Program, and so on. No matter what the program, letter knowledge, print awareness, reading, writing, talking, singing/rhyming, and playing are usually included. Melanie gives extensive background on the ECRR program in Chapter 4. The doodads described in this chapter should augment one or all of these activities.

Note: throughout this chapter I include three types of bulleted material.

- Book Suggestions
- ➢ Literacy Activities
- ✓ Doodad Factoids—assorted comments

Most families probably begin a literacy doodad accumulation of their own, and I would bet that it starts with a set of letter magnets on the refrigerator. At workshops, I always ask if the participants had ABC magnets on the fridge when they were little. Lots of hands go up. Often librarians mention that they have them on the refrigerator in the library's break room.

You might think that plastic letters with small magnets attached have been around forever. They seem to be readily available. I was impressed to learn that toymaker Fisher-Price introduced them in 1972 as part of the School Days Play Desk. A portable box with a handle, it had a magnetic chalk board on the outside and came with a tray holding 16 letters and 10 numbers, 16 stencils, and chalk. This fun-filled toy hasn't been produced for many years, but nostalgic fans can find pictures of it online and even purchase vintage sets from eBay and other sources.

So much for a brief history of letter magnets. What else fits into the category of Literacy Doodads? I've got lots of examples. You could say I have compiled a collage of them. Perhaps a plethora. Maybe a multitude. How about agreeing that I have a caboodle of oodles of doodads? See if you can imagine ways to use some of mine, and (probably) come up with more of your own.

## ALPHABET LETTER MAGNETS

I've found these in dollar stores and toy departments and even among kitchen wares. The title of this chapter was inspired by the cover of a kids' book. The title appears on the upper freezer section door and is spelled out in letter magnets. Here's the plot: a family of magnets (the Shivers) gets trapped inside a refrigerator. Will they escape their chilly fate? There are several other books that feature ABC magnets, and in the last four books listed next, they're the characters. Sometimes both upper- and lowercase letters appear. These books provide a great activity for a child to do alone (or with help) using letter magnets to re-create some of the illustrations.

- *The Shivers in the Fridge* by Fran Manushkin, illustrated by Paul O. Zelinsky (Dutton Books for Young Readers 2006)
- *Alphabet Adventure*, *Alphabet Mystery*, and *Alphabet Rescue*, all by Audrey Wood, illustrated by Bruce Wood (The Blue Sky Press 2001, 2003, and 2006, respectively).
- *The Sleepy Little Alphabet: A Bedtime Story from Alphabet Town* by Judy Sierra, illustrated by Melissa Sweet (Knopf Books for Young Readers 2012).
- Alphabet magnets turn up regularly in virtually every *I Spy* riddle book by Jean Marzollo (published by Scholastic).

Here are some other uses for magnetic letters:

➢ Tracing, doing rubbings, pressing into Play-Doh, matching, and sorting.
➢ They come in handy in display cases—along with an array of alphabet books, or to spell out words.
➢ Use them for signage—assemble the phrase you want then snap a photo. Try them for web pages, small signs in libraries, and do-it-yourself (DIY) greeting cards. Check Pinterest and Google Images.
➢ If you don't have a big collection of magnetic alphabet letters, the computer font called Calibri matches the ABC magnets' look, and you can make each individual letter in a different color. After printing them out, mount them on lightweight adhesive magnetic sheets found in office supply stores.

Some words of advice: to avoid frustration, purchase several sets. Watch for both upper- and lowercase letters. And remember: magnetic letters don't have to go on the refrigerator . . . they also stick to cookie sheets, pizza pans, and filing cabinets!

# BALLOONS

Whenever I did a literacy workshop (for parents, caregivers, and/or librarians), I wanted the participants to know right away that they were going to have fun while I modeled some techniques to enhance early literacy and make reading opportunities memorable and enjoyable for all. I always started the workshop with balloons. If the audience wasn't too large I tried to have enough "twist & shape" balloons blown up in advance so that everyone who was willing to take part could have one. These are the balloons that magicians and clowns use to make balloon animals. They're usually available in party supply stores.

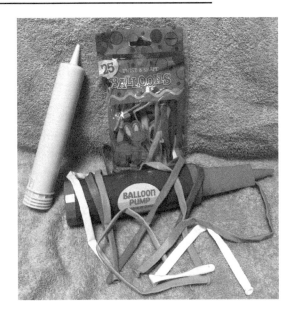

Here's some balloon etiquette to keep in mind:

✓ Balloon Phobia—This is real. There's even a name for that fear: *globophobia*. I've had folks get up and stand by the wall when I do this part of my presentation. Maybe it's the squeaky sound, or the potential of a balloon popping. For whatever reason, encourage people to opt out of this activity if they are uncomfortable.

✓ Latex Allergies—Also real. My director insisted that I include the fact that latex balloons would be used in my workshops on all promotional material.

✓ Balloon pumps are a necessity if you don't want to end up with a headache or worse from all that heavy breathing. Always use a pump! These often come with an assortment of balloons and sometimes instructions for making balloon animals.

✓ Roll enough of the balloon onto the tip of the pump so a knot can be tied easily.

✓ Don't fill the whole balloon with air. Leave a couple of inches near the tip to allow for expansion as the balloon is manipulated into shapes.

✓ I've never used balloons during an actual storytime . . . too many variables. But sometimes there have been small folks in my workshops, just because the parents had no childcare. So, this next piece of balloon etiquette is important.

✓ Balloon pieces can be choking hazards. So, if one pops be sure to pick up all the pieces and put them in your pocket, not a trash can in a public area where a toddler can fish them out.

✓ Large black plastic trash bags are perfect for transporting balloons to the site of your presentation and, coincidentally, conceal the balloons until the time to use them.

I like to use the balloon activity as an ice-breaker, especially if I'm facing a group that doesn't know me and may be apprehensive about the whole "Early Childhood Literacy" concept. Sometimes people get so involved manipulating their balloons that they turn it into a game and team up to spell words. Or they cooperate to make letters like X, H, or T. Big fun!

If you're not a clown or magician, you might not have a balloon in your pocket. But you might have . . .

## SHOELACES AND MORE

I demonstrate the shoelace doodad to parents and caregivers as a handy item to pull out in a situation where they are sitting and waiting for something . . . doctor's office, restaurant, and so on. Depending on the age of the child you're with, you can form a letter shape. Even better, let the child make a letter for you to guess. I like to ask workshop members if they have any ideas which letter might be a child's favorite. Invariably someone will say "M for McDonald's!" But we usually agree it's the youngster's initial . . . they've probably been seeing that most frequently from a young age.

➢ Something else that works great for letter shapes is yarn. When I do this presentation, I pass around a baggie of pre-cut lengths of yarn. Each participant takes one, and then the kids make letter shapes on the table in front of them, on their lap, or on the carpet.

> ➢ Pipe cleaners can also be used for this activity . . . they're super portable, and if you have several you can make more than one letter.

The thing to remember with all these activities is "Quit while you're ahead"    in other words, stop doing it while the youngster is still interested. And of course, don't let them get the impression that you're trying to *teach* them something.

After you've used the yarn idea a few times, don't be surprised if the children start to improvise. Here's a true story: a family visiting a sushi restaurant was worried about their five-year-old who was a picky eater. While everyone scanned the menu, the youngster amused himself by using chopsticks to form letters on the table. The waiter brought more chopsticks so that everyone could get into the act. All happily passed the time until their meal arrived. Extra bonus: the letter-maker decided to try sushi for himself and has become quite a fan.

Speaking of spontaneous letter-making, the youngsters in these photos used Jenga pieces creatively. Benjamin admires his H, and Phoebe has formed both upper- and lowercase letters to complete her name.

The items and activities I include in this chapter can be enjoyed by early readers of all ages . . . they're not just for kids. Adults struggling with literacy might be inspired by one "doodad," and it might be their key to solving the "mystery of the letters."

What else can you manipulate into letters?

# FOOD!

What comes to your mind first? Cooked spaghetti and licorice strips almost beg to be shaped into letters . . . and of course you can find lots of alphabet-related cookies, pasta, cereal, and so on. Food doodads may be as near as your own kitchen pantry, or they might require a field trip to the grocery store or farmers' market.

> ➢ Alphabet cookies are a fun way to do an activity called "Letter of the Day." Have the child pick a cookie from the store-bought bag or box and make that your "letter of the day." If S is chosen, you can start a dialog with questions such as "S—do we know anybody whose name begins with S? What animal begins with S? What do we wear that begins with S?" The letter of the day can also be chosen via Scrabble pieces, blocks, letter beads, or even a deck of flashcards. Or you can vary the method of selection every month or so to sustain enthusiasm. If the child goes to school, ask the child if he or she heard anything starting with the letter of the day after he or she gets home. Check Google or Pinterest for images of alphabet cookies.

➢ You can also use alphabet cookie cutters to make your own. Several brands and sizes are available. I found them in Walmart and stores that sell kitchen gadgets and supplies. You don't have to be Martha Stewart to have fun using these. Alphabet cookie cutters and Jell-O Jigglers can also be used on molded Jell-O. Use less water than called for in the recipe and keep the layer shallow.

➢ Small (less than 1 inch) metal cutters lend themselves to edible monograms. Even the pickiest eater would enjoy pressing his or her initials out of thinly sliced cantaloupe, watermelon, apple, or pear to make a name-kebab on a wooden skewer. Garnish

a personalized sandwich or pizza with letters cut from bologna or cheese slices. Cupcakes or other desserts could be embellished with letters of rolled-out fondant. Can you spell C-H-E-F?

Turn a grocery-shopping trip with children into an expedition to hunt letters of the alphabet. There are lots of foods that contain the letter O . . . cereals and cooked canned pasta . . . but they don't allow for much creativity. Instead look for alphabet cereal, soups, and canned pasta containing *all* the letters. Don't forget the candy cake-decorating ABCs along with tubes of icing for further letter fun. These are usually found near the boxed cake mix and canned frosting. Dry pasta letters and macaroni and cheese are awaiting you and your child in the grocery aisles.

> ➤ Put a spoonful of (uncooked) alphabet pasta onto a paper plate and have the child sort the letters—all As, Gs, and so on. Have them find the letters of their name or put them into alphabetical order!

Speaking of alphabet soup, Martha, the family dog, gains the power of speech after the letters in some alphabet soup wind up misrouted to her brain instead of her stomach in a whimsical series of books, which have also been turned into an animated series on PBS.

- *Martha Speaks*, *Martha Calling*, *Martha Blah Blah*, and many more, all by Susan Meddaugh (Houghton Mifflin Harcourt starting in 1995)
- *Alphabet Soup* by Kate Banks, pictures by Peter Sís (Dragonfly Books 1994) Knowing how to spell using the letters in your soup takes skill. Activity—re-create the words in the soup spoon using alphabet pasta. Refer to the beginning of the book to figure out where the characters come from.
- *Caillou: My First ABC: Alphabet Soup* by Anne Paradis, illustrations by Pierre Brignaud (Chouette Publishing 2015). While waiting for their too-hot soup to cool off, Caillou and his dad play a letter game. Discussion topic: What if the three bears' breakfast food was *alphabet soup* instead of porridge? How might that have changed Goldilocks's reaction?

Who doesn't love pancakes? Get ready for a stack of fun family food activities. Depending upon the age of the children, they can help read the pancake recipe, dictate or write out a grocery list of ingredients, go to the store and find each one, match the name on the container to the word on the list, then go home and start cooking! (Or take a shortcut and use pancake mix.) Having tried the activity in preparation for this chapter, I can share my personal pancake pointers:

- ✓ Search "pancake alphabet letters" on Google or Pinterest for examples.
- ✓ Put the batter in a squeeze bottle and "write" the letter with batter onto the pan or griddle.

- ✓ Use Goldilocks's trial-and-error method to find what's "just right!" Not too skinny, not too thick, not too small, not too big, not too raw, not too burned.
- ✓ Be satisfied making just a few letters to enjoy the experience, and then use the rest of the batter to make free-form pancakes that can be personalized with letters written in syrup.
- ✓ Alternatives: put more *fun* in this experience by trying *fun*nel cake. I saw a mix at the store that included a pitcher for pouring the batter. If waffles are more your speed, use chocolate chips, raisins, or blueberries to monogram them while they're still warm from the toaster or waffle iron.

Tie in books such as the following, either before or after you cook up a pancake event:

- *If You Give a Pig a Pancake* by Laura Numeroff, illustrated by Felica Bond (HarperCollins 1998). You're going to need syrup.
- *Cloudy with a Chance of Meatballs* by Judi Barrett, illustrated by Ron Barrett (Simon & Schuster 1978). Whenever I see the first illustration in this book I get a craving for pancakes. Grandpa is a flipping genius.
- *Rhinos Don't Eat Pancakes* by Anna Kemp, illustrated by Sara Ogilvie (Simon & Schuster 2015). Caution: do not invite a purple rhinoceros to breakfast!

Look on Pinterest for amazing alphabets and fonts made from just about any food item you can imagine. Cooked spaghetti, bacon, fried eggs, pancakes . . . this would be a fun activity for an older child, teen, or adult who is learning the alphabet. They could print out several alphabets, cut them up, and then do sorting, mix 'n match, or games of their own creation. Such folks could even start their own Pinterest pages, collecting interesting alphabets, fancy letters, and so on.

Browsing in a kitchen wares/baking section, I found a one-piece silicone mold to make 0.75-inch ABC letters. The label suggests that it can be used to create chocolates, candy, and even ice! The flexible silicone allows for mess-free release. It's safe for use in oven, microwave, fridge, and freezer—temperature resistant from 0°F to 400°F. One group of librarians described their experience making alphabet crayons with this mold, using shavings from broken crayons. This could be done at home with child helpers and lots of supervision when using the grater and the oven.

The activities I describe involve lots of talking and vocabulary building as positive side effects. Some would work in a library setting, but many of them are more suitable for the home. Remember, the goal with everything I've talked about is to be Teaching without Preaching. And of course, the art of it is not to appear to be *teaching* at all!

# WALL DECOR

Having alphabet letters in the home environment is another subtle way to reinforce letter knowledge. Any craft store or even Walmart is a good place to start. Spell out a child's name or his or her favorite team on a wall or shelf. Window- or wall-cling letters can be easily

repositioned or removed. Various fonts are available in wood, plastic, metal, cardboard, and so on, both flat and 3D.

Alphabet posters are great room or library decor. I love seeing pictures of library activities on Facebook or YouTube and spotting some alphabet posters that I may have used myself. Publishers often offer these as freebies at library conferences.

> ➢ It would be a fun activity to make a wall display of photos of people making balloon letters.

## PLACEMATS

I've collected alphabet placemats from a variety of sources: dollar stores, teacher supply stores, Walmart, and so on. They generally include upper- and lowercase letters, plus illustrations of things that start with each letter. Many are laminated and reversible and allow for coloring with dry-erase markers. My favorite placemat features the sign language alphabet. I mounted it on the end of a bookcase in my library. Children frequently stood in front of it either alone or with a friend and practiced the gestures. It was so popular that I left it behind when I became literacy coordinator. I was delighted to find the poster again in a museum gift shop. Aside from the obvious use of placemats prior to or during meals, they have many other uses. Following a brainstorming session at a caregiver training session, I compiled the following activities:

> ➢ Put the placemat on the floor and toss a lightweight object such as a coin onto it. The tosser then must name something (such as an animal, an article of clothing, a type of food) that starts with whatever letter the coin lands on.
> ➢ Blindfold children, give them a sticky dot, and guide them to an alphabet placemat mounted on the wall. When they remove the blindfold, and see what letter their sticker landed on, they must think of a word that starts with that letter.

➢ Pass out placemats and dry-erase pens to each child. Have a race to see who can be first to circle the letters of their name. Other similar search-and-find games could be substituted for names, since Ed might always win, while Charlotte was still hunting.

➢ Since the placemats are inexpensive, a child can be encouraged to look for them when shopping, and a variety can be collected. Put them in rotation to avoid boredom.

# BEADS

Alphabet beads come in all shapes, sizes, and materials: round, square, plastic, wood, foam, metallic, glitter, and even "glow in the dark." I found a bag of letter-shaped pony beads, all capitals, but was dismayed that there wasn't a single E in the sizable assortment. I needed to spell out the word "BEADS" using real beads for a photo/label on a PowerPoint slide. For a moment, I thought I'd have to go back to the store for more. But after pushing the beads around with my finger I discovered that an upside-down G closely resembled a lowercase e. Saved by improvisation! Plus, a clever tip to mention to the viewers of the PowerPoint.

✓ Doodad Factoid: I love the chance to be creative putting together letter items and then snapping photographs to use in presentations, for signs, and on social media. I've done it with many of the doodads I describe. The first photo in this chapter showcases this technique. Here's the key: D—wooden alphabet block; O—Haribo gummy candy alphabet letter; O—plastic magnetic letter; D—thin cardboard magnetic letter; A—thick foam alphabet puzzle piece; D—pony bead letter; S—thin foam letter game piece. Assorted small letter beads are scattered in the background.

# FANCIFUL LETTERS

I've already mentioned the importance of a child's initials when fostering letter recognition. But the whole initial/monogram idea lends itself to literacy doodads. Consider the "drop caps" used as a design device in the ABC Books chapter of this book. Expand that concept to the fancy letters found in illuminated manuscripts. Many of these have intricate details featuring flowers, animals, and other designs. Imagine asking older children or teens to create a fancy letter to appear in their own illuminated manuscript. What things might they include inside the letter to describe their own interests? Since drop caps and letters in illuminated manuscripts are pretty small, use a large letter outline as a starting point for an individual's personalized version. Think of it as an autobiography in graphic form contained in the shape of the letter. Pinterest and Google Images provide inspiration. Books of fairy tales often contain elaborate dropped caps. Look for the elaborate O in "Once upon a time . . ."

## RUBBER STAMPS

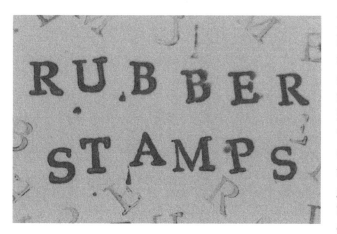

I had a set of alphabet rubber stamps as a kid, and I loved playing with them. Maybe that was one of the things that led me to a career as a librarian! Rubber stamps seem to have become obsolete in libraries. The last time I recall using one was to stamp "Damage Noted" and then handwrite the date on the inside front cover of a book that contained some scribbling. A little girl wanted to check it out but was afraid that she might be blamed for doing the coloring.

ABC stamp sets are great gifts that can double as art supplies for a somewhat older child. I found sets of letters as small as about 0.25 inch in size. Several fonts are available, both upper- and lowercase, serif and sans serif. There's even one that looks like typewriter keys (round black circles). Stamp pad sizes range from 2-inch square on up, in a rainbow of colors. Look for these (and all my doodads, really) in craft stores, Walmart, dollar stores, and online.

✓ Doodad Factoid: I get e-mails from Jo-Ann Fabrics and Michael's that always contain discount coupons, so if I have the patience, I can wait to buy stuff when I can get it for 40 percent or 50 percent off.

## LETTER AND NUMBER PUNCH SET

I happened to see these for sale at Costco a few years ago and bought two, one for my daughter, the teacher, and one for me. At that time, I wasn't doing early literacy training and workshops, but I was a children's librarian and used this a lot for craft activities, signs, and so on. They came in their own case, and each punch contained a tray to catch the letters. You just pried it open and took them out.

The neat thing about punches is that you end up with a "positive and negative." When you punch out a word you have the loose letters (such as C-A-T), which would be the positive. The piece of paper that the letters were punched out of is the negative and can be placed over a contrasting color.

✓ Doodad Factoid: if you see something like this and think you might have a use for it sometime . . . buy it! It probably won't be around by the time you realize you can't live without it.

# BOARDS

Here's something else that isn't always available . . . often they only show up around back-to-school time. A DIY project would be to purchase some chalkboard paint and make your own. Take your pick from high tech and low tech.

➢ Dry-Erase Boards—These come in all shapes, even a paddle, plus they come with lines or designs or in color, often with pens and even magnets on the back. These are great for letter practice, or just scribbling, so little folks can practice fine motor skills involved with holding a marker.

➢ Scribble Slate/Magic Slate/Magic Tablet/Neon Slate—These come with a stylus for scribbling/writing. Lift the clear top sheet and the writing disappears. They consist of stiff backing, a lightweight plastic sheet, and a clear or tinted heavier plastic cover sheet.

# IT'S TIME FOR A DOODAD ANECDOTE

One of my colleagues, Natalie, left three-year-old Cameron with grandma several afternoons each week. From the beginning, their regular routine involved watching *Wheel of Fortune*. Grandma kept a small dry-erase board nearby on an easel. Once or twice during each show, when a contestant would call for a letter, Grandma was ready. If the contestant said, "Is there a C?"—and indeed Vanna White turned around a C—Grandma wrote a C on the board, saying "Look, Cameron! See the C? Can you say C? Your name, Cameron, starts with C!" If a player decided to buy a vowel, "Is there an E, Pat?," and there was indeed an E to be turned around, Grandma wrote an E. Grandma might remark, "E! Can you name an animal that starts with E?" She and

Cameron were playing their own game. But Grandma was smart. She didn't do many different letters in one day. If a letter turned up during the same episode, she might mention it. This letter fun activity happened whenever Cameron was at Grandma's and *Wheel of Fortune* happened to be on TV. Over time she gave Cameron a small dry-erase board and pen, so they could both write down letters. Grandma didn't make a huge deal of the game; it was something that she and Cameron had fun sharing. At some point, Natalie was running errands with Cameron. They pulled into a parking space, and Cameron piped up from the car seat, "H—O—B—B—Y L—O—B—B—Y: Hobby Lobby!" Startled, Natalie turned around and said, "Cameron! Where did you learn that?" And Cameron replied, *"Wheel of Fortune."*

I love telling this story. I include it whenever I do a workshop. I've also shared it casually with folks who know I have a fascination with early literacy if they ask me for ideas they could try with their babies, toddlers, or grandchildren. It's perfect because it includes several early literacy techniques, but doesn't come across as "teach-y." There is letter repetition, both by sound and by sight. There is writing practice. There is talking: the dialog between Grandma and Cameron. This scenario can be easily modified, too. More than one child can be involved, and various ages can take part. An older sibling could fill the Grandma role. It could become a family activity. A chalk board could take the place of the dry-erase one, and participants could jot down their own letters on scratch paper. Part of the fun is devising different ways to do the basic activity. A good chance to play "What if . . .?" What if *Wheel of Fortune* comes on at an inconvenient time? What if we have the capability to record it and watch when we want? What if we "pause" the show while we search scrabble tiles, alphabet blocks, magnetic letters, or cookies to match the letters in the puzzle? How simple is the concept of using *Wheel of Fortune* as a fun and easy way to build early literacy skills? Yet how far-reaching are the results?

The Doodad Story about Hobby Lobby and the sign on the building leads to the next topic.

## ENVIRONMENTAL PRINT

When I started keeping my eye out for signs to photograph for my PowerPoint presentations, I was really struck by how we are constantly bombarded with words no matter where we are! Surely a kid riding along in a car must notice this stuff, unless he or she has his or her nose in a video game! (If he or she has his or her nose in a book, however, that's okay.) Running errands in the car is an excellent opportunity to watch for the "Letter of the Day" or the child's initial, and so on. Another thing to try and spot while driving around is letters on license plates.

## FLASHCARDS

These are a fun way to learn letters, keeping in mind that you don't want to overdo it. Always stop before the child becomes bored. Again, these can be found in dollar stores as well as Walmart and teacher supply stores.

✓ Doodad Factoid: when I suggested DIY flashcards at a parent workshop one of the moms said, "Why would I spend the time making my own when I can get them at Dollar Tree for a buck?"

That comment led to a fun discussion of how to make your own flashcards, with the overwhelming majority suggesting getting the children involved. They could do whatever parts of the project they were capable of. Make it a family activity and remember to check Pinterest and Google Images for ideas.

Cut pictures from magazines, newspapers, junk mail, or even packaging. How about a set based on logos of familiar stores or products? (M for M&Ms, O for Oreos, and so on.)

➢ Outline the letter on each card with Puffy paint to make the letter three-dimensional. Kids could trace the letter with their finger to reinforce the letter's shape: tactile learning! Similarly, ask a person to close his or her eyes while you "trace" a letter in the palm of his or her hand. There's also the fun of tracing a letter or word on a person's back and seeing if he or she can figure out what you've "written."
➢ Cut letters from sandpaper and mount them on cardboard for more tactile learning.
➢ Make a set of flashcards for the 26 letters of the alphabet using a deck of cards—put capital letters on the black suits (clubs and spades); lowercase letters on diamonds and hearts.

Speaking of cutting pictures out of magazines or newspapers . . . I found a great set of board books at Dollar Tree a few years ago. It was one of those lucky events that you can never count on. Currently they're available only via third-party sellers such as eBay or Amazon. Search term: Crayola Big Book.

• *The Big Green Book, Big Yellow Book*, and so forth. Published in 2011 by Dalmatian Press/Greenbrier in Franklin, Tennessee.

There are four separate books: green, red, yellow, and blue. Each is die-cut in the shape of a crayon. They measure 15-inch long by 3.5-inch wide. It's fun to pick one up and ask a child to guess what might be inside. Imagine how they might answer if they were looking at the yellow cover. They're usually surprised at first, and then fascinated, to see yellow things—bananas, a canary, a workman's hard hat, a jar of mustard, and so on.

➢ It would be fun and easy to make similar books, looking through newspapers and magazines to find different-colored items. Cut them out and keep them in separate baggies or folders, then paste them into a notebook or scrapbook. Neatness isn't a priority. The point is to have a creation that means something to you and that you enjoy looking at.
✓ Doodad Factoid: Are you a thrifter? Thrift stores are an excellent source of Literacy Doodads. You never know what you might discover. Once I snapped up a set of board books, 2.5-inch square, one for almost every letter of the alphabet. They're great for small hands to open and "read" and can also be used as toys. When I found them, it was obvious they had been well loved. I got a set of 25 for $2.50. They look great in display cases. In fact, I took a photo of them to use in the ABC Books chapter.

# PUZZLES

Whether they're foam, wood, jigsaw, or something else, alphabet puzzles provide fun and painless literacy practice.

> ➢ Toss a few foam alphabet letters into the tub to simulate alphabet soup.

I've gotten years of use from a large foam alphabet and numbers puzzle mat from Costco. I bought one for my library and one for myself. I used it in at least two storytimes per week for the six years in a branch library, where I was the children's librarian. Each individual piece is a 12-inch square. I still use some of the letters when I model a storytime as part of my early literacy presentation. I hold them up one at a time before I announce the theme. I show the first letter and say, "What letter is this?" Audience responds, "P." Next, I say, "Does anyone have a name that starts with 'P' . . .? Can you name an animal that starts with 'P' . . . ? How about a color that starts with 'P' . . .?" Then I bring up the I and ask similar questions, then link it to the P. Then I hold up the Z . . . same routine. Then I show the second Z . . . right away the kids notice that the second Z is really an N turned sideways. This leads to a fun dialogue about the fact that my alphabet set has only one of each letter. I describe how sometimes

librarians must be creative. I always ask them if a sideways N looks enough like a Z for us to use it. Luckily, they agree, and we can move on and add the A. When they are all linked together, I say, "What does it spell?" And everyone shouts "PIZZA!"

This is an example of how you can play with letters . . . Sometimes I'd say "Imagine if I were doing a storytime with a theme that called for another duplicated letter? What if I was doing a storytime about MOMS? What could I use for the second M"?

- The centerpiece of my pizza-themed storytime is *"Hi, Pizza Man!"* by Virginia Walter, illustrated by Ponder Goembel. Originally published by Orchard Books in 1998, this fabulous book had been out of print for several years but was brought back by Purple House Press in 2017. It is fun to read, has an excellent assortment of animals, calls for audience participation, contains the "what if . . ." questions, and leads to lots of pizza talk.

I keep the book concealed inside an actual pizza box, and it doesn't become visible until I first tease the children by lifting up the lid a little bit and saying, "Can you smell the pizza? What does it smell like? Cheese, pepperoni, mushrooms?" Next, I ask if they'd like to bake a pizza. Then I read a poem that I have taped inside the lid:

- It's the title poem from a collection of humorous poetry on a variety of topics: *A Pizza the Size of the Sun* by Jack Prelutsky, pictures by James Stevenson (Greenwillow Books 1996).

When I first did themed storytimes, I would comb the Internet for songs, fingerplays, and poems based on whatever theme I dreamed up: teddy bears, chickens, pigs, cats, and so on. I printed them out and stashed them in folders, to be pulled out once a year or so. When

I revisited my pizza materials in preparation for this book, I noticed that I hadn't kept track of where I had found them originally. Since I couldn't be sure of copyright, I'm not providing them in this chapter. But I was amazed to find virtually every poem, song, and fingerplay on what I consider Ali Baba's cave: Pinterest. Instead of saying "Open Sesame!" I just enter appropriate search terms. What fun! We always ended pizza storytime singing and acting out the Pizza Pokey. I would ask the children to suggest their favorite toppings. And, you guessed it . . . the words to Pizza Pokey are on Pinterest, along with the P-I-Z-Z-A song based on B-I-N-G-O.

I would also have on display and available for checkout as many books about pizza as I could round up. I would include picture books, chapter books, fiction and nonfiction, plus cookbooks. Below are a few of my favorites:

- *The Little Red Hen Makes a Pizza* by Philemon Sturges, illustrated by Amy Walrod (Dutton Books for Young Readers 1990)
- *Pete's a Pizza* by William Steig (HarperCollins 1998).
- *Hold the Anchovies!—A Book about Pizza* by Shelley Rotner and Julia Pemberton Hellums, photographs by Shelley Rotner (Orchard Books 1996).
- *Everybody Loves Pizza: The Deep Dish on America's Favorite Food* by Penny Pollack and Jeff Ruby (Emmis Books 2005).
- *Pizza: How to Make and Bake More Than 50 Delicious Homemade Pizzas* by Carla Bondi (Readers Digest third printing edition 2011)

Let's look at some more assorted doodads.

## SCRABBLE LETTERS

It's not necessary to purchase a brand-new set to get these classic finger-friendly wooden game pieces. Scour the toys/games section of a thrift store (or the toy area of a garage sale). Even if the set is incomplete, you'll probably still have a good assortment of ABCs. There is also a kid's version of the game with the letters on heavy cardboard squares. Cheez-It Scrabble Junior crackers make a tasty snack too! Keep in mind that these letters can spell out words for signage, labels, and so on. Generic letter squares (without number values in the corner) turn up in craft stores too.

## ALPHABET BLOCKS

Talk about variety in material, size, color . . . take your pick! And, they're great for building (fine motor skills again!). Speaking of building, spend some fun minutes looking up Lego Blocks or Lego Letters on Pinterest. Make that an hour.

- Having a problem keeping your blocks together? Read *The Letters Are Lost* by Lisa Campbell Ernst (Puffin Books 1999)

# SCRAPBOOK PAPER

There are tons of designs with alphabet letters in the scrapbooking section at the craft stores.

➢ For a fun family project, each member could make his or her own set of letter magnets thanks to the variety of patterns in both upper- and lowercase. Adhere them to a lightweight magnetic sheet (available in office supply stores). Don't miss the ripple effect of this activity, starting with the trip to the craft store to choose the paper, then actually making the magnets over one or two home sessions, playing with them, putting messages on the fridge or pizza pan. It would be like sending text messages, without using a phone or computer.

➢ Gift wrapping paper often features ABC letters, as do gift bags and greeting cards. Be a cutup! The letters can go on magnetic backing, or glue them to felt for use on a flannel board.

➢ Fabric is another source of alphabet fun. I had a simple reversible vest with two different letter patterns that I wore for storytimes and presentations.

# STENCILS

Like all the other doodads previously described, stencils come in a wide variety of styles. They could be one piece with all letters; sets of individual letters (script or block letters, upper- or lowercase); sets with letters and other shapes such as animals.

# STICKERS

There's an endless variety of ABC stickers, ranging from bags or tubs of adhesive foam letters to sheets and pads of paper ones. This brings up another Doodad Anecdote.

One time I thought I'd found a goldmine with a tablet of 20 identical sheets that contained both upper- and lowercase letters, plus numbers. And, it cost less than a dollar. Luckily, I didn't snap up all the packages.

Taking a closer look at the stickers a few days later, I mentally picked out the letters to spell my name: Kk, Aa, hmmm . . . no Tt. And no Yy. In fact, the letters stopped after Q. No little q. No more letters at all! Numbers filled out the rest of the page. No way to spell Kathy. Imagine if I had given out these sheets to a group of youngsters. Chances are many of them would have been disappointed or frustrated, maybe even stressed out, if their name contained R—Z. What did I learn from this? I learned to pay attention when I'm shopping for doodads. If only I had sung the alphabet song when I first picked up the sticker pad, the music would have stopped short. But I've gotten my money's worth out of these stickers, because at every workshop and presentation I show them as an example of just how important reading/literacy is. I relearned that lesson when I bought several packages of plastic alphabet letters at a dollar store. They looked just like the magnetic alphabet letters I had purchased elsewhere. Except they had no magnets! Sure enough, the package just said, "Alphabet Letters," not "Magnetic Alphabet Letters," which appeared on the packs I had at home.

# ABC BOOKS THEMSELVES!

Certain alphabet books qualify as doodads. Look for ones that feature a large outline of a letter and contain a variety of items. Often those items all begin with the particular letter. I recently found an ABC book that could best be described as an I Spy alphabet on steroids! It's called *I Spy ABC: Totally Crazy Letters!* by Ruth Prenting, illustrated and designed by Manuela Ancutici (Firefly Books 2017). Each letter fills almost the whole page. The fascinating part is that each one is made up of an artfully arranged jumble of things. But not just random things. The C is composed of things you might find on a walk in the woods: leaves, seed pods, rocks, berries, pine cones, and even a snake skin! N is a collage of art supplies: stencils, erasers, pens, paints, brushes, crayons, paint chips, and even pencil sharpeners. My favorite is Z. The components are postage stamps. This book was originally published in Germany, and the stamps are from all over the world.

- ➢ Often at a thrift store or garage sale you can find a big jar or cigar box filled with broken costume jewelry, incomplete decks of cards, golf tees, orphan puzzle or game pieces, or other surprises. Imagine a group of teens who are struggling with literacy poking through those items and filling in the shape of their initial. (Actually, this would be a compelling craft with practically any group or individual, but as a literacy activity it's definitely thinking outside the [cigar] box!)
- ➢ Why not make it a fun family project for all ages: maybe grandpa or a favorite uncle has a collection of fishing lures or flies, or military insignia (medals, uniform buttons, patches, or insignia). Bring out Auntie's stash of buttons. (Or maybe Auntie is the one with military insignia and fishing gear!) The possibilities are limitless.
- ➢ Sharing a book this detailed with an older sibling or a family member who might recognize something often triggers a memory that leads to a story. And what component of ECRR is this? Talking! Not to mention vocabulary building.

# LETTERS, LETTERS, EVERYWHERE!

An episode of *Antiques Roadshow* featured an embroidered sampler that was a family heirloom. In recent years, samplers have become important in museum collections as representations of early American female education. Not only was a sampler a good way to learn various embroidery stitches, but it was also an early Literacy Doodad! Create your own family heirloom. Find inspiration on Pinterest: search heirloom sampler or cross stitch alphabet.

## ARE YOU FEELING AN ATTRACTION TO MAGNETIC LETTERS YET?

They don't just belong on the fridge!

> ➢ V is for Vase. The trick here is to have two vases (glasses, actually): one small-diameter one that fits inside a larger one. The letters are slipped between the two glasses, and then water and flowers go in the inner glass. This technique could also be used in a clear lamp base as a decoration in a child's room.
> ➢ Alphabet letters look very elegant when spray-painted gold.
> ✓ Doodad Factoid: many of the items I have described are small and might pose a choking hazard: as always, be aware of this and use them appropriately.

## THE MAIN THING TO KEEP IN MIND WITH ALL THESE LITERACY DOODADS IS TO HAVE FUN

Speaking of other early literacy skills . . .

## HERE'S A SUPER DOODAD TO ENHANCE SINGING!

We all know the connection between singing and early literacy—it subtly demonstrates that words are made up of syllables and helps with memorizing. Has anyone ever forgotten the alphabet after learning the ABC Song (which is sung to the tune of *Twinkle, Twinkle, Little Star*)? And it's fun!

Librarians sing in storytime, or in an early literacy workshop, or at a presentation (even if we're not that great at singing). We do it because we're modeling the behavior for the parents or other audience members. They figure, "Well if *that* person can do it, I certainly can!"

Have you ever struggled with beginning a song and realizing you started either too high or too low to carry off the entire tune? Investigate Boomwhackers, lightweight, hollow, color-coded, plastic tubes, tuned to musical pitches by length. These are great in storytime and would have many uses in a family setting as well.

Pinterest and Google Images are a wonderful resource. It's fun to look for things related to early literacy, using terms such as letter crafts, preschool alphabet, alphabet crafts, alphabet activities, and preschool letters. I've pinned a lot of my favorites onto a board I named Literacy Doodads. Many of the things mentioned in this chapter are there. I'm constantly adding new stuff. There's only one disadvantage: items cannot be easily rearranged or categorized (it has something to do with "tiling"). And items don't appear in the same order every time. This is a small inconvenience compared to the value of Pinterest. Happy hunting!

I know from experience that getting parents and caregivers to come to a workshop on early literacy can be difficult if not impossible. "Maker Stations" programs in libraries for kids or kids and parents have become popular. I bet that "Literacy Stations"—programs aimed at parents and caregivers—would be a hit. Attendees could try out some of the doodads in this chapter. Handouts of the library's early literacy activities, literacy tips, booklists, and more would be provided. "Stations" could include DIY flashcards, crafts with alphabet pasta, rubber stamping, and a big selection of ABC books to look at/check out.

## ONE LAST DOODAD ANECDOTE

I've given literacy workshops and presentations for a wide array of audiences over the years, but the most personally rewarding were the sessions I conducted at the Bernalillo County Detention Facility. I was invited by an English instructor whose students were working on their GEDs. Since many of the inmates were parents or grandparents, or had very young family members, she thought a presentation on early literacy tips would appeal to her group. In advance, I submitted a detailed outline of my workshop and the materials I would be bringing in. I was allowed to demonstrate all my literacy doodads except the one that involved balloons, which was nixed. My library provided me with a variety of books of various reading levels—board books, picture books and chapter books—and each attendee was able to select one to keep. I did two presentations, back to back, for female and then male inmates. The students were extremely attentive. The two comments that made the biggest impact on me came at the end of the programs. A male inmate came up to me and said, "A lot of the ideas that you've shown us are just common sense— and when you described them I said to myself, 'Why didn't I think of that?' But I probably would never have thought of them without your suggestions. Thanks so much for giving us these valuable tools!" The second comment I'll never forget came from a woman who spent several minutes looking over the selection of free books. She finally picked one up and hugged it. It was a bilingual lullaby board book. She came up and whispered, "I have a new granddaughter who was just born last weekend. I know I will love reading this book to her. *Gracias!*" I was moved by her words for several reasons. For one, she certainly didn't look old enough to be a grandma. Secondly, I knew some obstacles the inmates faced. Although family visits were allowed at the facility, these had to be conducted by video. No in-person contact was permitted. I'm sure that this woman would be motivated to read to her granddaughter no matter what, and to this day I envision her cuddling that baby/toddler/

preschooler/kindergartener in her lap and sharing books. I get the same feeling when I hear about members of our military who are deployed overseas but make the effort to Skype or video share reading with their youngsters. Sometimes we take for granted the ease with which reading can be fostered. Stopping to consider the lengths to which some people will go underscores the vital importance of literacy.

# REFERENCES

Banks, Kate. 1994. *Alphabet Soup.* Peter Sís, illustrator. New York: Dragonfly Books: Distributed by Random House.

Barrett, Judi. 1978. *Cloudy with a Chance of Meatballs.* Ron Barrett, illustrator. New York: Simon & Schuster.

*The Big Green Book, The Big Yellow Book, The Big Red Book, The Big Blue Book.* 2011, Franklin, TN: Dalmatian Press/Greenbrier.

Bondi, Carla. 2011. *Pizza: How to Make and Bake More Than 50 Delicious Homemade Pizzas.* New York: Readers Digest.

Ernst, Lisa Campbell. 1999. *The Letters Are Lost.* New York: Puffin Books.

Kamp, Anna. 2015. *Rhinos Don't Eat Pancakes.* Sara Ogilvie, illustrator. New York: Simon & Schuster.

Manushkin, Fran. 2006. *The Shivers in the Fridge.* Paul O. Zelinsky, illustrator. New York: Dutton Books for Young Readers.

Marzollo, Jean. Various Years. *I Spy Riddle Books.* New York: Scholastic.

Meddaugh, Susan. 1992. *Martha Speaks.* Boston: Houghton Mifflin Harcourt.

Meddaugh, Susan. 2013. *Martha Blah Blah.* Boston: Houghton Mifflin Harcourt.

Meddaugh, Susan. 2013. *Martha Calling.* Boston: Houghton Mifflin Harcourt.

Numeroff, Laura. 1998. *If You Give a Pig a Pancake.* Felica Bond, illustrator. New York: HarperCollins.

Paradis, Anne. 2015 *Caillou: My First ABC: Alphabet Soup.* Pierre Brignaud, illustrator. Montreal: Chouette.

Pollack, Penny, and Jeff Ruby. 2005. *Everybody Loves Pizza: The Deep Dish on America's Favorite Food.* Cincinnati, OH: Emmis Books.

Prenting, Ruth. 2017. *I Spy ABC: Totally Crazy Letters!* Manuela Ancutici, designer and illustrator. Buffalo, NY: Firefly Books.

Rotner, Shelley, and Julia Pemberton Hellums. 1996. *Hold the Anchovies!—A Book about Pizza.* New York: Orchard Books.

Sierra, Judy. 2012. *The Sleepy Little Alphabet: A Bedtime Story from Alphabet Town.* Melissa Sweet, illustrator. New York: Knopf Books for Young Readers.

Steig, William. 1998. *Pete's a Pizza.* New York: HarperCollins.

Sturges, Philemon. 1990. *The Little Red Hen Makes a Pizza.* Amy Walrod, illustrator. New York: Dutton Books for Young Readers.

Walter, Virginia. 1995, 2017. *"Hi, Pizza Man!"* by Virginia Walter, Ponder Goembel, illustrator. New York: Orchard Books. Cynthiana, KY: Purple House Press.

Wood, Audrey. 2001. *Alphabet Adventure.* Bruce Wood, illustrator. New York: Blue Sky Press.

Wood, Audrey, and Bruce Wood. 2003. *Alphabet Mystery.* Bruce Wood, illustrator. New York: Blue Sky Press.

Wood, Audrey, and Bruce Wood. 2006. *Alphabet Rescue.* Bruce Wood, illustrator. New York: Blue Sky Press.

# Chapter 3

# Dynamic Displays: Minimum Work, Maximum Impact

Libraries often have a display case or curio cabinet that contains more cobwebs than collections. Sometimes they also have a blank wall that could easily be filled with fun. Displays can contribute to literacy in so many ways. They foster creativity among staff members and can involve community members as well. This chapter includes:

- Lots of ideas for book-theme displays, based on many years of putting them together in a variety of settings
- Photos and descriptions of crowd-pleasing, inexpensive, and not-too-labor-intensive displays that will inspire readers to try new methods of grabbing the attention of their patrons (young and old)
- Clever wall designs that can stay up through several seasonal and holiday changes with minimal work
- Jazzy display case tricks designed to draw viewers like a magnet
- Ideas on how to convince collectors to share their treasures!

Since an effective display is a great way to promote literacy, emphasis will be placed on incorporating books into the scenario.

I've always been attracted to displays in libraries. Not just book displays and bulletin boards but especially items displayed in locked glass cases that you can get really close to without touching them. There was a multilevel case in Mesa Public Library when I was growing up in Los Alamos, New Mexico. I always made a beeline for it when I visited the library. The displays were changed frequently and invariably sparked my curiosity about whatever new items were featured. My childhood library no longer exists. There's a newer building in a different location. But my beloved display case is now downstairs in the Children's Room, and I make a point of seeing what's in it whenever I return to my home town.

I think that childhood experience of being exposed to new things helped me realize that learning (and literacy!) can be encouraged indirectly. Sometimes the information we pick up in this way can be more memorable and motivating than something we are told (or taught) by a parent, teacher, or librarian. As we know, there are many ways to learn! As I mentioned in my Doodads chapter (chapter 2), a youngster (or adult) might not respond to a flat poster or book in a display. But if there is something three-dimensional (3-D) beside it (like a dinosaur or a robot or some artificial flowers or something sparkly) . . . their eyes are caught, and they come in for a closer look. An extra advantage of displays is that they're on the job all the time. They can be explored at the convenience of the viewer, and if they're well done they explain themselves.

I started doing displays of my own during my first library job, in the Air Force Library at Andersen AFB, Guam. The display case was a window built into a wall that could be accessed only from the librarian's office. It faced out into the entrance area of the library next to the circulation desk. There wasn't much room in the case, but it did have a couple of narrow moveable shelves and an area at the back to mount flat materials. The constraints of the small space made coming up with interesting displays a real challenge.

This picture shows the display case area that I had at my first library job with Albuquerque Public Library. The case was in front of the window in the Manager's Office. The window provided me with lots of extra real estate on which to display flat items. It was located near the magazine section and on the way to the restrooms, where there was plenty of foot traffic. Once a display was in place, I put related books on clear cubes on either side of the case. These books were checked out at a fast clip, so I would request duplicate copies to be sent over from other branches in our system. Keeping books available was crucial to complete the goal of the display: to encourage kids and adults to check out books that were related to whatever was going on in the case.

Also shown here is a version of my December display. Gingerbread and the Nutcracker Ballet alternated as the theme from year to year. The big gingerbread man is a window cling, and the smaller ones surrounding him are from a deck of cards. Various gingerbread items filled the case, including ornaments, socks, dolls, houses, cookie cutters, gingerbread tea (Celestial Seasonings), notecards, and a couple of garlands of sparkly plastic gumdrops. I attached gift bags filled with tissue paper to the wall by the case. This photo was taken before I had a chance to put out the books.

That window was a real decorating bonanza that provided a large area to show off fun stuff. One of the most popular displays I ever did was for the Day of the Dead/*Día de los Muertos*. I taped an almost-life-sized flat cardboard jointed skeleton onto the glass from inside the Manager's Office. The bony holographic fellow came from Dollar Tree. I'll mention here that whenever possible in this chapter I'll tell you where I got many of the things I describe. (Also, full disclosure, *I do not* own stock in Dollar Tree—but there's a Dollar Tree in my neighborhood!) Back to the window: the other dancing skeletons were printed on brightly colored paper. I cut out the parts and tied the joints together with loops of thread so they could be posed. There are several jointed skeleton templates available on Google Images and Pinterest. Once all the skeletons were in place, I lowered and closed the blinds that provided a plain backdrop and gave the manager her privacy.

You may be wondering why I chose to do a display for Day of the Dead/*Día de los Muertos*. For starters, it's super colorful and attractive. The celebration is observed in Mexico as well as regions with large Hispanic populations and has been the subject of two recent animated films: *Coco* (2017) and *The Book of Life* (2014). This joyful holiday focuses on gatherings of family and friends to pray for and remember friends and family members who have died. I've been fascinated with it since I returned to New Mexico in 1994 and have collected a lot of related items. *Día de los Muertos* usually falls around October 31–November 2, but celebrations are also often held on the weekend nearest those dates. I liked to put up this display in mid-October. Since it features a cultural theme, I preferred it to doing anything connected with Halloween. Frankly, I felt a Halloween display case might invite challenges. Don't get me wrong, we had tons of books about Halloween in the library and usually started putting them out in our "holiday books" area in the Children's Room at the beginning of October. In fact, I did receive a challenge about a Halloween book. The book in question was *The Halloween Handbook: 447 Costumes* by Bridie Clark and Ashley Dodd (Workman Publishing 2004). You can read about my experience in *True Stories of Censorship Battles in America's Libraries*, edited by Valerie Nye and me (American Library Association 2012). Look for the chapter called "The Ghost of Halloween Past."

The display case shown in the previous photos had a hinged lid that opened from the front for easy access. The lid of the case was very heavy, and luckily there were two metal arms that helped hold it open. (Fortunately, it also featured a lock.) I always worked on my cases in the hour before the library opened so I didn't have to contend with lookie-loos who might cause the lid to come down unexpectedly with dire consequences. I liked to spread stuff out around me, so I could choose what items to include, and it would have been impossible to keep track of everything if patrons, especially little ones, were nearby. Prominently featured was a jointed tin skeleton that echoed those on the windows. I suspended small jiggly skeleton key chains from the inside lid of the case. When the case was closed they seem to be floating in space, giving kind of a 3-D effect and providing shorter viewers something special to look at without having to be picked up. When starting a display, I used various boxes and sometimes a plastic periodical case underneath some type of drape to add height on which small items could lean or rest. I accumulated several drapes over the years, including lengths of fabric and tablecloths. I kept a note with the dimensions of the case in my wallet in case I found a remnant that might make a perfect drape for a future theme. Using the boxes to add height ensures that all dimensions of the case, width, length, and depth, are used. Other Day of the Dead items that jazzed up the case included postcards and greeting cards, a candleholder, a potholder, fabric, a necktie, a crepe-paper flower head wreath with lots of ribbon streamers, and plenty of painted skulls. I bought the skulls at Michael's—a dozen small ones came in a net bag, and I had fun decorating them with paint and sequins . . . I can imagine teens doing a skull craft workshop. Sparkly items help catch people's eyes, so I often used metallic "shred" (the kind used in gift bags) that comes in lots of colors (Dollar Tree again). I also sprinkled in a path of yellow petals from inexpensive artificial flowers to represent the trails of marigold petal that families make to help departed souls find their way.

I realize a Day of the Dead display might not be relevant to your particular situation. I've chosen to describe mine to convey some universal techniques that can be used in any display . . . sparkles such as sequins and shred, boxes underneath the fabric "base" of the display to add height and variety, plus a wide array of different items. I was always amazed when people would come up to me and say that I must have added stuff to the case after I first launched it. They just hadn't noticed those things the first time, which led to return visits!

Now for something completely different . . . Guess who's having a birthday? Or an Un-Birthday! Her name is Alice. A few years ago, we decided to throw a Mad Mad Tea Party at our branch. Our posters and invitations included the lines:

Wear a costume when you come: Tweedledee or Tweedledum . . .

Caterpillar, Talking Flower, Queen of Hearts with all her power.

Wear a hat, any style will do. The Cheshire Cat will smile at you.

We'll celebrate our Un-Birthdays . . . in lots of "Mad" but funny ways!

The poster featured some of the original illustrations by John Tenniel found on Google Images. Lots more of them are available now following the 150th anniversary of the publication of *Alice's Adventures in Wonderland* by Lewis Carroll, which was observed in 2015. Also available are characters from the 1951 Disney cartoon movie.

Several staffers in our branch were tea aficionados, and they were willing to share their tea party paraphernalia. I made available for checkout as many books for kids and adults on tea and tea parties as we had in the library, along with various versions of Alice books.

Here are some details on what went into the case: playing cards double-stick-taped to the back wall of the case, fancy teacups on a raised platform, a plastic mushroom, and flamingo stir sticks. A remnant of white lace added a touch of elegance over a portion of the blue satin drape. Sharp-eyed viewers could glimpse a black mouse in a white teapot. I cut out a Disney Alice from a sheet of scrapbook paper from Jo-Ann Fabrics. Small hearts, clubs, diamonds and spades, also from a scrapbook paper sheet, were scattered around the case. It was a tea party, so I included a golf tee. A Cheshire cat smiled on the "Celebrate" postcard put out by the U.S. Postal Service in 2005, along with a Mad Hatter and Alice stamp. (Fun fact: first-class postage

for a letter then was 37¢. Lots of commemorative postage stamps came out for Alice's 150th anniversary. Look for them on Google Images!) An actual Twinings tea bag was included along with various diffuser implements for use with loose tea, pink spoons from a box of Sweet'n Low artificial sweetener, a mug with Disney Alice characters, and a silver and white mushroom clipped to a small mirror. (Note: the tag on the teabag becomes important in the I Spy Tea Challenge described later. Think "twin.") Shortly before I did this case, McDonald's Happy Meal came with dolls of characters in children's books, and I was able to snap up Alice and the Mad Hatter. A coworker brought in a Christmas tree teapot, which looked stunning on part of a lacy red shawl near the back of the case. (Note: shawls, lace, doilies, napkins, placemats, etc. add interest and variety and don't take up too much space. Be creative!) In addition to a cookie cutter shaped like a teapot, I had TEA spelled out in Mary Engelbreit letters from Michael's. (In my Doodads collection, I have a lot of different plastic, foam, and cardboard alphabet letter sets, Scrabble letters, alphabet beads, and so on that can be used to spell out the theme of a case . . . and conveniently provide letter recognition for early readers!) I found a deck of clear playing cards in a magic shop. They were perfect for this theme, but if some day you're going to be hosting a magician, you could use the cards in a display case about magic tricks (with an accompanying display of books on "How to Do Magic Tricks"). Don't forget to put in a stuffed rabbit and the *most* magic card of all . . . a library card!

You're probably wondering what Alice-related items I put in the big window. I used more playing cards on it, along with what had to be the most unmanageable croquet mallet ever! Reminiscent of the jointed skeleton, I found a jointed flamingo in the luau section of Dollar Tree. I didn't put any floaters in this one, figuring that the short folks would have plenty of other things to look at. I often use small rocks, erasers, pencils, and so on under flat items so that they stick up at an angle. This adds dimension to the overall display plus makes the flat things easier to see for youngsters and people in wheelchairs.

Since the *I Spy Riddle Books* were (and still are!) so popular, I treated this case as a real-life I Spy Tea Challenge. Here are the words, which were posted on the window above the case:

Use your mind, use your eye. Read the riddles, Play I SPY!

Careful. This one's pretty hard: The Queen of Hearts . . . on a CARD!

Look for a tea cup with roses blue. Find the word "twin" (this one's hard too!)

A cupcake with an orange butterfly. (Hint: A silver tray's nearby.)

Listen . . . Can you hear the purrrrrr of two Cheshire cats with orange or pink fur?

I also spy a Christmas tree, plus Tweedledum and Tweedledee.

Do you see a looking glass? Through it Alice had to pass.

A tiny mouse his time is biding. (In a tea pot he is hiding!)

Take your time and find a tee. A postage stamp is filled with glee.

I made a handout with all the challenge items listed along with a box next to each one, so viewers could check off each one they found. Children often brought parents over to see if they were as good as their kids at spotting things, and plenty of teens seemed to have fun making a group effort to "SPY!" Based on your own themes and items, make up your own

I Spy challenge! Caution: folks may expect you to create an I Spy Challenge for every display, which can turn into an excellent opportunity to draft teen volunteers!

I've gone into detail on the case descriptions hoping that some item I mention may trigger a memory of something you have stashed away that could be the nucleus for a future case. I did a Dr. Seuss case every year for "Read Across America" around March 2 (his birthday), and many staff members had Seuss stuff to share. Lots of Seuss material is available at the World of Dr. Seuss website (www.seussville.com)—I liked to show the URL prominently, so parents and caregivers could look up more stuff if their youngsters were interested. The recipe for Green Eggs and Ham is on the Seuss website, and it was a no-brainer to slip two green plastic eggs from an Easter assortment into the case. My manager was a big fan of the Cat in the Hat. She had a collection of CitH items, which was the core for my case. Figurines, rubber stamps, socks, a commemorative stamp first-day cover, t-shirt, and so on. For extra zaniness, I liberally sprinkled colorful pony beads, paperclips, hair ties and mini-rubber bands throughout the case. (All items from Dollar Tree). We always put vast quantities of Dr. Seuss books adjacent to this display and replenished them several times a day. We requested books from other branches that weren't going quite as far as we were to celebrate this major event! A booklist of Dr. Seuss titles makes a nice handout, and it can be embellished with Dr. Seuss characters from the Internet. Kids were always fascinated by the photo of Dr. Seuss/Theodor Geisel. Often, they said he looked like the Cat in the Hat, or maybe a smiling Grinch. They loved this quote from Dr. Seuss:

You're never too old, Too wacky, too wild . . .

To pick up a book and read to a child!

Several years later when I became literacy coordinator for the system, I recited this poem every time I did an early literacy workshop for parents, grandparents, and caregivers. I also included it on a handout.

The subtitle of this chapter on displays is Minimum Work, Maximum Impact. And one of the features is that they're *not too labor intensive*. Most of the work on the display cases I've been describing goes on before the actual setup. You will probably spend the most time collecting items that you want to include in the case and obtaining plenty of books that go along with the theme. It's handy to provide a booklist handout so that folks who didn't get to check out the display books the first day can remember to look for them later. The actual setup of the case goes fairly quickly. Put the underlying shapes in first, followed by the background drape. Then comes the FUN! You can play with the objects, finding the best possible arrangement. Once the display is up and you notice people looking at it, take advantage of the opportunity to talk to them (especially the kids) about the various items. Ask what their favorite thing is, point out the related books or booklist, and so on.

Then comes the time to start thinking about what you want to display *next*. Taking down a display usually goes even quicker, and once the case is empty it's perfectly acceptable to put in a sign that says, "Watch this space for an exciting new display coming soon!" if you don't have something new ready to install. Leaving a case empty for a short time helps build suspense and excitement and may even lead to suggestions of what could go in next.

Looking for inspiration?

➢ Most important, take the time to record the measurements of your display cases, bulletin boards, or other wall areas for when you're out shopping and happen to run across something that might be perfect for your needs. The remnant bin at a craft store is a great source for drapes to go in cases!

➢ If you're lucky enough to have a bookcase to devote to a display, and staff to tend it, an Author Birthday theme is quick and easy. There are lots of ways to go with this, but for basic information I rely on the Perma-Bound Author/Illustrator Birthday Calendar. Usually available at library conferences, this valuable resource can also be found online at www.perma-bound.com/author-illustrator/. Be sure to print out a copy of the calendar for folks to refer to near the display. They can find out what writers share a birthday with them and also look up their favorite authors. Keep shelves stocked with works by that month's authors. This idea could also be adapted for the teen and adult areas of the library.

➢ Is there a cultural festival held in your area every year? A weekend of Dutch Days, or maybe a Greek, or Polish, or Irish, or Italian celebration? Somebody in town no doubt has a collection of related mementoes and souvenirs that they would be delighted to show off in the library.

➢ Other display case themes that people might have items to share include Wizard of Oz, Harry Potter, Eric Carle (could be combined with a ladybug collection or a variety of insect-related items). Star Wars, Wonder Woman, and Curious George are some other fun possibilities.

➢ Does your library have a knitting/crochet group? How about a Lego Club? If not, perhaps community members who are real Lego enthusiasts might lend some of their works of art and even do a program! One of the most popular exhibits in the Home Arts Pavilion every year at the New Mexico State Fair is the Lego Creations.

➢ If you're in a school setting, perhaps staff members would take part by offering to lend you part of a personal collection of McDonald's toys, Beanie Babies, postcards, baseball cards, old tools, and so on.

➢ Let's not forget thrifting (garage sales, Salvation Army, Goodwill, animal shelter thrift shops, and more!). Seasonal items usually appear just after they're current, but they can also turn up throughout the year. If you keep your eyes peeled, you just might find the perfect centerpiece for your next display!

# CLEVER WALL DESIGNS THAT CAN STAY UP THROUGH SEVERAL SEASONAL AND HOLIDAY CHANGES WITH MINIMAL WORK

When I went to a new job at a branch library I was challenged by several large expanses of blank wall. The walls were plaster with a woven fabric covering, so staples could easily be removed and didn't leave marks. Pushpins worked great too. For the smaller wall, I came up with an idea based loosely on the Tree of Knowledge. For the background, I cut a long strip of blue craft paper (comes in various colors on large rolls). Using Con-Tact paper with a knotty pine design from Dollar Tree, I cut out a tree trunk and branches. My first use of the tree was around back to school time. I found artificial apples at a thrift store. The leaves of the tree were small green plastic plates from Dollar Tree cut into pie-slice sections . . . when mounted on the wall they stuck out like real leaves. I also put in some leaves cut from two shades of green bond paper. I added the phrase "Harvest a Bushel of Books." At that time, I used a low-tech lettering system . . . letters were connected to one another using brass brads. So many more lettering systems are available now, including die-cut alphabets and endless fonts on the Internet. I put books about apples, harvesting, and back to school under the tree on the long shelf, which was the top of our storage cabinets.

In October I added orange plastic pumpkins (thrift store) and a pumpkin garland from Michael's. Also a few ghosts. The library's Halloween books were displayed below.

Our library had a set of posters for every month, and such things are still being produced. I used a poster that said, "Scare up some Good Books!" Poster sets and bookmarks for every month of the year are readily available from outfits like Upstart and Demco. Your library may already own some. If not, check out their websites to get ideas. You might not even have to buy anything!

For November, I took down the green leaves, apples, and pumpkins and added leaves made of orange, yellow, and red plastic plates. I also added some brown ones made of brown construction paper and brown paper bags. A jointed turkey from Dollar Tree personified the phrase "Gobble Books." Thanksgiving books were displayed below.

For winter, only a few brown leaves clung to the branches. Staff members cut snowflakes from white copier paper and holographic wrapping paper (super sparkly!). They also made giant snowflakes using newsprint end rolls that I bought very inexpensively from the *Albuquerque Journal*. Teen volunteers can be happily tasked to cut out snowflakes, taking into account the geometry involved in folding and cutting a six-pointed flake. This could count as a STEAM project (Science, Technology, Engineering, Art, and Mathematics). I wish I had taken pictures of the giant snowflakes that we used on our windows. We left them up for several months, adding some seasonal embellishments (heart doilies, shamrock cutouts, etc.). Let this be a lesson to you: take pictures of all your displays! They might come in handy at a future interview, or you might even include them in a book some day!

The phrase for the winter wall was "Snowflakes and Books—Endless Variety." There was a sparkly snowflake garland bracketing a strip of snowflake-patterned paper along the bottom of the tree. I cut the words "Endless Variety" out of the snowflake paper. We never had an actual "Christmas" display, although we certainly put all the Christmas, Hanukkah,

Kwanzaa, snowmen, and so on books out in an easily accessible area.

➢ Save as many physical items of your display as possible so they can be used again in another library. I used the snowflake lettering cut from wrapping paper on a smaller bulletin board several years later. It went into an empty frame outline on the wall, and I used part of a blue plastic tablecloth for the background. This comes on long rolls in a variety of colors at Party City, and Dollar Tree also sells pre-cut plastic tablecloths in solid colors.

Recently, I received a publisher's e-newsletter with the subject "Differences."

The first sentence of the message was: "Books—and stories—are like snowflakes. Or opinions. Or perceptions. Each one is different. And we pride on ourselves on finding those different-ish things and bringing them to you. You're welcome! This week's newsletter is about diversity in books." Diversity . . . a really hot commodity these days . . . perfect subject for a winter bulletin board? It was fun to see this message since I had featured snowflakes and endless variety on a bulletin board I made over 15 years ago!

For February, I used plastic heart ornaments (thrifted!). Portraits of all the presidents graced the tree as well. I used a pretty labor-intensive process of photocopying their pictures from the encyclopedia. But now those are readily available on the Internet. Even easier would be to cut up a poster of all the presidents that vendors give away at library conferences. In February, the tree had no leaves yet. Too cold! The phrase used was "Be a Book Lover!" Valentine books and presidential biographies were displayed.

➢ Pushpins facilitate hanging the heart, apple, or pumpkin ornaments I've described earlier. The loops slip right over the pushpins. These are available in colors as well as clear plastic . . . If you're not sure what I'm referring to, there is one featured prominently on the cover of *Paper Towns* by John Green.

In March, birds are nesting. I crumpled a brown lunch bag into a nest shape with raffia strips for comfort. I cut some owls from an old poster, and smaller birds were sitting on some of the letters in "The Early Bird Gets the Books."

Spring at last! Light green leaves appeared on the tree, along with pink blossoms made of tissue paper and pink cellophane. A kite motif said, "Soar with Books."

And all of a sudden . . . it was a Summer Reading Fiesta! Darker green plastic plates were cut into pie slice shapes, light green paper was snipped into leaves, sunflowers from Dollar Tree were pulled off their stems, and their leaves were used on the tree too. Holographic

discs in rainbow colors and sparkly yellow buds made from cellophane crumpled into balls rounded out the summer tree.

I left the branch library where I had created the tree, and, not surprisingly, when I was assigned to that building again several years later, the tree had been "weeded" (a little library humor, there). But that large expanse of bare wall was still crying out to be filled. As I mentioned, we didn't do specific "Christmas" displays, but we looked for other winter holiday themes. A variety of performances of *The Nutcracker* take place in Albuquerque every year from mid-November through Christmas Eve, and many staff members had some type of Nutcracker stuff, so we were set.

I had a large cardboard nutcracker that had been part of Borders Books Holiday decorations the previous year. (I had used my connections to get them to give me one when they got ready to take them down.) It sat on the shelf below the wall on which I mounted flat items such as greeting cards, placemats, gift bags, and stickers. I adapted my technique of jamming the display case with so many eye-catching items that people just can't avoid stopping to look. A wall full of interesting items was unusual enough to attract attention. There were plenty of nutcracker and ballet books nearby for ease of checkout.

> ➢ Don't be afraid to ask local stores to save their seasonal promotional materials for you when they're no longer needed. I know of several libraries that do this regularly. I think the best "treasure" that I ever saw was a life-sized model of Dobby the House Elf, which a librarian friend of mine scored when theaters were promoting whatever latest Harry Potter movie was coming out. I've since seen artifacts from *Star Wars* and other blockbuster movies that have book tie-ins.

On a huge bare wall in the programming area of the library I used sparkly holly garlands to bracket a huge assortment of nutcracker gift bags filled with crumpled tissue paper so they stuck out from the wall.

# If You Give a Mouse a (Gingerbread) Cookie, She'll Want to Decorate It (Again and Again)!

The best big-wall decoration I ever came up with involved elaborating on the gingerbread display case I had elsewhere in the library. I enlarged a basic gingerbread couple to make them 36-inch tall and cut three pairs out of light brown paper. The eyes, mouth, rick-rack trim, and pink cheeks on the girl were basic. The first year I dressed them in red and green buttons, ribbon neck bow, and hat. A star was attached to a cord they each held. These guys stayed up only until after Christmas. The following year, I brought them out again. They began the season holding a handmade snowflake, and their buttons were light blue and white, with a paper-punch snowflake on each one. Blue, white, and silver ribbon added style to her neck and his beanie.

For February, a heart-shaped doily was added to each snowflake, providing a lacy Valentine. The buttons were changed to pink and white with a paper-punch heart on each one. Headgear was a linked-hearts tissue paper garland, and the bows and skirt trim were rose-printed ribbon.

In March, a shamrock cut from green paper replaced the heart doilies on each snowflake, although I have since seen shamrock-shaped doilies that would be cute too. Dollar Tree had green and white leis, so I took one apart and used the flowers to adorn the buttons and embellish the skirts. Glitter foam shamrocks in two shades of green adorned the heads.

For spring, flowery paper plates and pastel-colored leis made perfect skirt trim, necklace, and buttons. Floppy ears added a whimsical touch. I haven't cropped this photo so you can get an idea of the scale of the room. There is a drop-down screen in the ceiling. Also shown

is my storytime chair and one of the carpet cubes that usually held the display books. The basic gingerbread couples were on the wall from December until April, when we took them down to put up Summer Reading Program decorations. Very little work went into changing them according to the seasons, staff members got involved suggesting clothing components, and patrons young and old loved seeing the new "outfits."

To emphasize the importance of saving decorations for possible reuse, here's a perfect example. A few years ago the summer reading program theme was "Every Hero Has a Story." Heroes of all kinds, from history, comics, movies, and especially real life, were featured in libraries. While researching the theme for some workshops I was going to do, I decided to include ninjas. Imagine my delight when a ninja gingerbread man popped into a "We found some new Pins for you" e-mail from Pinterest. Clothing was easy, a black covering from head to mid-body, with a narrow strip on the face for the eyes. I made a small "Ninjabread Person" to demonstrate as a craft project and showed a slide of my wall-sized gingerbread couples, suggesting how cute they would be in ninja garb. Since there are plenty of ninja books, folks were excited to grab this idea. Don't be afraid to hang on to your creations if you have the storage capability. Some might call this "hoarding," but I prefer to refer to it as "archiving." Who knew that *gingerbread* would morph into *ninjabread*? As I said, "If you give a mouse a cookie" . . . she might even turn it into a Wookiee. Don't believe me? Proof is on Pinterest.

I bet that teen volunteers would enjoy helping out the library by making large wall decorations. I used a grid to scale and enlarge the original gingerbread couple I found on the Internet. Unless you have access to an overhead projector, the grid method of scaling and enlarging is very easy to do, and the results are super satisfying. And you can tailor your results to a specific area and make them as gigantic as you like. I used this process many times for various wall installations. Teens might get a kick out of this "low-tech/ retro" technique, and the fact that there are YouTube videos showing how it's done would add appeal. Extra bonus: since there is *math* involved, not to mention graph paper, rulers, yardsticks, and teamwork . . . it's really science-y!

Looking for a really easy idea for enhancing a problem area, or even cover a stain, dent, or crack? Our OPACs (Online Public Access Catalogs) were mounted on a nifty stand that reminded me of a breakfast bar. It was located at the entrance to the Children's Room, so it provided an eye-catching welcome. The front featured an ingenious wood-framed, cork-backed area, while wiring and some storage were accessible from the back. I loved using these. They provided a fun challenge and were exciting for the kids. Plain paper or seasonal wrapping paper could be stapled onto the cork to provide a background to which wording and decorations could be added. Scalloped borders added a finishing touch and covered up any crooked edges. This technique could be adapted to brighten up narrow vertical spaces or other problem areas. Use scalloped borders from Dollar Tree or office/teacher supply stores. They come in an almost infinite variety and are so versatile.

The best thing about displays is that they're fun—for both the creator and the viewers!

You may never know the impact of your displays unless you get feedback from your library patrons. And this adulation may not come right away. I've often had children or parents remark to me several years later that they just loved coming to the library during the December holidays to see the gingerbread display. One youngster who was in high school confided that he had been fascinated by the Day of the Dead case when he was little—the jiggly skeleton keychains were right as his eye-level and made quite an impression! He asked his mom to check out one of the display books on the skeletal system (a nonfiction one), which kindled an interest in anatomy that he had kept up ever since. The leg bone's connected to the knee bone; the display case is connected to the literacy bone . . . This gives a whole new meaning to the term "boning up" or studying, in a good way!

## REFERENCES

Clark, Bridie and Ashley Dodd. 2004. *The Halloween Handbook: 447 Costumes.* New York: Workman Publishing.

Nye, Valerie and Kathy Barco, editors. 2012. *True Stories of Censorship Battles in America's Libraries.* Chicago: ALA Editions.

# Chapter 4

# Musical Storytimes Build Literacy Skills

I am hoping this book will inspire first-time storytellers or even those that have been doing them for a while and want to try something new. At conferences I start by saying, "If I can convince you to even think about incorporating an instrument into your storytimes, I have accomplished my goal."

## WHY DO STORYTIMES?

To understand something about my connection to storytimes, read the following thank-you note given to me in December 2016:

> Dear Melanie,
>
> The word library is synonymous with your name. I say "library," and Nico [18 months] says, "Melanie." Thank you for all that you do to make the library such a wonderful place to be. It's a favorite part of our week to be at your storytimes.
>
> Warmly and lots of gratitude,
> Nico, Felix [new baby] and Pam

I believe *wholeheartedly* that the reason I connect with children and their families is that I have fun. The literacy education is important—making it *fun* amps that importance up!

How do I do that? I continually grow and learn from my coworkers, other storytellers, performers, and most importantly, the children. My theme is "let the child lead." A coworker taught me how to be a storyteller, and she always told me, "Think about how long a child has been in the world. What is their experience? What do they know?" It isn't fun if the kids and caregivers are not connecting to the literature. In my all-ages storytime, where the average child is three years old, I won't read a book about going to elementary school. If I'm reading a book and notice a child getting uncomfortable, I'm going to tone the book down. If I'm reading a book and notice many of the kids loving it, I'm going to amp it up. But after everything I have learned through my years of storytelling, one of the main ways I've learned to connect children to literature is through music, through singing, and using real instruments—playing them and letting the kids play them.

## A LITTLE ABOUT ME

I was educated in music, theater, and English. I have my BA in English and theater from the University of Utah. I have my MS in English from Utah State University. I worked in a bookstore through college and then got a job in a small library close to where I was getting my master's degree in Logan, Utah. I also took classes at Weber State University, mainly because they had a great musical theater program and I love musicals. I once had a storytime dad describe me as "Someone that wanted to be in musical theater, but just couldn't make it on stage. She's too much of an introvert." He's right; in theater classes, I would always hide in the back, watching everyone else on stage and reading every script I could. I wanted to be a stage writer. So yeah, I wanted to be in musical theater, but while it was too much for me to be on stage, I so love the literature!

It seemed library work, specifically in youth services, was the perfect combination of what I wanted to do with my life. I get to be around books and express my voice, drama, and musical-instrument knowledge (limited as it is) through storytimes.

At my first library job, in 1998, I started doing storytimes and loved it. It was easy for me. I could find a written/illustrated story and bring it to life. However, I also noticed the profound connection I was making with small children. I noticed that it is not just the literature; it is engaging a child through multiple formats like books about all sorts of topics (nonfiction and fiction), flannels, songs, and so on and thus finding that link to literacy. A child comes through the doors of the library in the hands of a caregiver. The librarian links that child to a bigger world through storytime and by making the library an accessible, fun place to be and to experience literature. I have caregivers tell me their children wake up wanting to come to storytime. The power of story is a timeless tool a librarian uses to connect a child to reading and writing. "The value storytelling holds as a source of inspiration and as a teaching tool makes it the most important tradition mankind possesses" (https://www.hslda.org/Contests/Essay/2013/Cat3/Carpenter.pdf).

After about a year, I had the opportunity to become a circulation supervisor at a branch, and because it was significantly more money, I took that position, but I missed working with children. After I received my master's degree in 2001, my husband and I decided to move to Boulder, Colorado. I applied and got a youth services library assistant position at the Boulder Public Library, and that is where I still am today. My job has changed to the title of "youth services scheduling specialist." I do four storytimes a week—two of those are specifically musical—and I also do the schedule for our department. I feel very lucky to be doing something I love.

So here we are. I want to give you some hints, script ideas, and specific things I do to inspire you to find what you are most passionate about in life and direct it into your storytimes to make you the best storyteller you can be.

# A LITTLE ABOUT MUSICAL STORYTIME AT BOULDER PUBLIC LIBRARY (OR MAYBE A LOT)

Here I will discuss how musical storytime got started. (I will talk about the theory behind why music is important for children later in the chapter.) My experience as a storyteller has really grown over the past 15–20 years. At the time I am writing this book, I incorporate songs and/or play the guitar in every one of my storytimes.

It all started doing singing stories in storytime. They were a natural transition for me because I always did fingerplays that incorporated songs. I would read books and then break up the reading with "Twinkle Twinkle Little Star" or "Eensy Weensy Spider" to involve the kids and get those fine motor skills going. The break of a song/fingerplay felt important to segue between the rhythm of a song and the rhythm of a book. I could engage some kids with pictures and reading and others with the fingerplays. When I started running across books that were actually songs, I really found my niche. One such book is *We All Sing with the Same Voice* by J. Philip Miller (HarperCollins 1992). I totally remembered this from my youth watching PBS's *Sesame Street*. I still love doing it for storytime. I love the message. When I incorporated it into my regular storytimes, the kids were engaged, and many caregivers were singing with me. It went over so well I decided to look for similar books.

I started to open each of my storytimes with a song book, read a few more books, do some movement, bring the kids back to more stories with another songbook, do a flannel or pop-up book, and then end with a song or another song book. I do a 45-minute storytime and still follow this outline. I do not use scripts for my own storytimes. I choose many books and let the children lead me from the books that I have. Sometimes we do many long books and little movement; sometimes we do two short books and all movement. I try to be ready for anything.

As far as musical storytimes and how they began, I blame it all on one of my favorite storytellers, Woody Guthrie. For his birthday one year, I decided to do all songbooks. I opened with *Bling Blang* by Woody Guthrie (Candlewick Press 2000) and cried through *This Land Is Your Land*, also by Woody Guthrie (Little Brown and Co. 1997). I can't remember all the books I used, but I did not stop singing once. I moved between flannels, movement, and books. I read and sang the entire storytime. It was exhausting, but it was so much fun! I had many compliments—people wanted more.

In the summer of 2009, the Collaborative Summer Library Program's theme was "Be Creative," and we decided to add some special storytimes that were all songs. It is a lot to do all singing books, and I found it was much easier with another person. My boss asked my coworker, Alice, to do a storytime that was mostly musical books once a month, but it was exhausting to keep up the level of energy needed to sing and act out each book for the full 45-minute storytime. Even though Alice's storytime day was not my regular time slot, we decided to try to do it together. We put together a storytime of songs where we took turns with each book or song. We called them musical storytimes, and we did two a month, taking the place of a regular storytime slot from each of us. It was extremely well received. One of the main comments we received was that children would stay focused for the entire storytime, even the babies!

In addition to the kids being engaged, the dynamic between the two of us went really well. The second person makes the storytime so much easier on multiple levels—I cannot stress this enough. I will talk about this more in the next section, "How to Create and Present a Musical Storytime."

We continued doing musical storytimes, and they became more and more popular. As the storytime grew over the years, it was becoming more of an institution and a regular program at the library. We would bring in new patrons for "music classes," as patrons would call them. Our average was 80–100 people. During the summer, we had school groups join us, and we would have up to 130 people!

At this point, we were incorporating musical instruments, but simply in a toy-like fashion. Alice and I would occasionally pull out all our instruments and we would parade around the auditorium.

After two years of musical storytimes going really well, something magical happened; a coworker donated her guitar to the library. Now, I played in college, but I was never very good. Still, I could step out of my comfort zone, and after some practice, instructions from my husband who plays, and many YouTube tutorials, I picked up that beautiful instrument and was blown away by the effect it had on my storytimes.

Of course, at first I did not dare to play. I would bring it out for my personal storytimes instead of musical storytimes. I would do one song and then put the guitar away. I started doing Toddler Times, and the guitar seemed to be a natural fit for that storytime. Our Toddler Times are smaller, and I go much slower. It is more of a lapsit program aimed toward the caregivers as much as the kids. They are also age-specific for children aged 24–36 months. (I talk about Toddler Times as part of Caregiver Storytimes in Chapter 5, "Themed Storytimes and Scripts.") I do a lot of repetition. So pulling out the guitar was easy. The kids *loved it*, as did the caregivers. I was overwhelmed at the amount of passion people show for a simple instrument. Think about that first time you heard *live* music. Not played on the radio, not just sung acoustically but your favorite song, played *live*. For me it was Howard Jones, 1985, the year I graduated from high school. Instead of my graduation ceremony, I went to see him live in concert. When he started playing the piano and played my favorite song, "Things Can Only Get Better," I was transformed.

At conferences, I tell the story about a very young boy who came up to me at the desk in the library and said, "par tar pease?" I had no idea what he meant, and I looked at his caregiver, but she didn't know either. He looked at my back office where I store my guitar, and it hit me that he was saying, "Play the guitar please." I went and got my guitar, and he smiled.

From that moment on, I knew that a musical instrument was key for me to create a connection with children and make storytimes (and more important, early literacy) fun.

I started incorporating guitar into musical storytimes regularly in about 2012. We would usually open and close with a guitar song. I became well acquainted with Jim Gill, Laurie Berkner, Raffi, and more. There are so many fun, fabulous songs, and really, you can find simplified guitar versions by simply searching the song and adding "guitar chords simplified." We always end with a song, and with a guitar it is so much easier! I know many of you reading this book have had a CD skip, or the iPod or your phone is not charged, or you cannot get the connection to work. All those unplanned technical difficulties that cause such a headache. With a musical instrument, you never have to worry about any of that (other than the occasional string breaking). It is basically fail-proof, except for user error, which you should *never* worry about because we have the least judgmental audience in the world: children! They get enough music played with computers and phones. How amazing is it to come to a library storytime and hear a *live* instrument! It amplifies what we are teaching and helps connect those children to what we are teaching them.

In 2014, our library underwent a huge redesign. The children's library completely moved. We were able to design the storytime space with musical storytime in mind. The architects incorporated acoustics, and we built a room large enough to accommodate bigger numbers but still felt like a children's area (not an auditorium.) The design included a complete sound system with microphones! How overwhelming is that?! Well, it was, and we shied away from using them for about the first year.

At this point, we decided to start doing musical storytimes once a week, instead of twice a month. We also added an afternoon storytime. We did a survey of what our patrons wanted in the afternoon, and overwhelmingly, that answer was another musical storytime. The best day was Thursday, but I already did Toddler Time in the morning, and after adding an afternoon musical storytime to that day, needless to say, I started to burn out. We hired Ruth, and she played the ukulele! I was ecstatic! Today, she and I alternate Toddler Times and do musical storytimes together. I have written more about the creation of this storytime in Chapter 5 "Themed Storytimes and Scripts."

# HOW TO CREATE AND PRESENT A MUSICAL STORYTIME

Now that you know how this all got started, let us discuss how to create and present a musical storytime—in particular, how to incorporate instruments to make it extra fun!

# EVERY CHILD READY TO READ (ECRR) AS BACKGROUND KNOWLEDGE TO PREPARE FOR STORYTIME

Before creating any early literacy storytime, you need information so you can make informed decisions about choosing materials. I am very thankful for ECRR and the wealth of knowledge it gives to educators and caregivers. ECRR was founded in 2004 by the Public Library Association and the Association for Library Services to Children. I have watched the program grow and expand throughout its use in conferences and libraries. It shifted my intentions for educating children to educating the parents too: "If the primary adults in a child's life can learn more about the importance of early literacy and how to nurture pre-reading skills at home, the effect of library efforts can be multiplied many times" (http://everychildreadytoread.org/about/). ECRR gives parents and educators skills for promoting early literacy. For me, learning those skills and seeing how they affect both the children and their parents led to the pinnacle of my discovery—that music is one major tool that makes these skills come alive, easier to understand, and more exciting!

After doing storytimes for about eight years, I trained to do Toddler Time using ECRR and the Six Skills, or ECRR 1: Print Motivation, Print Awareness, Vocabulary, Letter Knowledge, Phonological Awareness, and Narrative Skills. These skills were developed for librarians to become more thoughtful about how they are teaching literacy in their storytimes. The skills are given to the caregivers but patterned through storytime for the children. This really expanded my skills as a storyteller. I was doing a lot of this already, but doing and thoughtfully creating are two completely different things. The Six Skills are very academic, which I liked, but when ECRR 2 was introduced in 2011 (the Five Practices: Play, Read, Sing, Talk, and Write), that was the perfect fix to make the Six Skills even more attainable! The simplicity of the Five Practices comes alive when partnered with the Six Skills. I will give many examples of both the Six Skills and Five Practices later in this chapter. Musical storytimes naturally evolved from these ECRR teachings.

I believe that three things are necessary for preparing a successful musical storytime: (1) choose books and flannels that are musically based, (2) incorporate instruments and let children experience them hands-on, and (3) have two storytellers present the storytimes.

## It's All about the Books

I cannot stress enough that if you want to be the best storyteller you can be, you must do your own thing. Do what speaks to you, what you love, or what you've seen children love. What I describe is how it works best for me.

I start by choosing musical stories. I use two types: **rhythmic books** and **songs done as picture books**. I mentioned a few in my background story. Here are more that I use and the how and why:

**Rhythmic books.** Books that are not a song, necessarily, but they have a fabulous rhythm (hello phonological awareness, but also print motivation, vocabulary, and all the rest, really.) There are *many* books. Here are a few of my favorites:

*I Got the Rhythm* by Connie Schofield-Morrison (Bloomsbury 2014)
This book works great with a senses storytime. Or even how to recognize rhythm everywhere. I do this with a drum and/or have the audience clap with me.
     You can see me read this book on Boulder Channel 8's *Read with Us*, Episode 1. https://boulderlibrary.org/youth/read-with-us/

*Hand, Hand, Fingers, Thumb* by Al Perkins (Random House 1969)
The classic indeed. A coworker suggested this book to me when I was looking for good books for my 18-month-old (who is now 16). Thank you, Margaret! You suggested a book that not only did my daughter love but also one that has become a cornerstone for me to show rhythm in a story. I do this with clapping or a drum and as a call and respond:

> Hand Hand Fingers Thumb
> One thumb One thumb Drumming on a drum.
> One hand Two hands Drumming on a drum.
> Dum ditty Dum ditty Dum dum dum.
> (Audience responds, "Dum ditty dum ditty dum dum dum")
> Rings on fingers.
> Rings on thumb. Drum drum Drum drum Drum drum drum.
> (Audience responds, "Drum drum Drum drum Drum drum drum.")
> And so on.

*Jazz Baby* by Lisa Wheeler (Harcourt 2007)
Works on many levels: loud soft, high low; it incorporates family and play. I clap a rhythm with the group, and I tap my lap or shoe while I read.

*Rain Makes Applesauce* by Julian Scheer (Holiday House 1964)
I did not dare do this book for a long time, because Judy, one of my mentors, used to do this book beautifully, and I did not think I could live up to her style. Nevertheless, I learned to read it my own way. (Although I do use her same tone when I say, "Oh you're just talking silly talk.")
     This is a great book to read rhythmically, but you can also reflect the humor in the text. I will even pause after some of the lines, if I am getting a reaction to how creative and funny the text is. For example, "Elbows grow on a tickle tree." Ruth will stop and say, "*What?*" Then continue with the rhythm, "And rain makes applesauce."

**Songs done as picture books.** By this I mean books in which the text of a song is written out as the text of the book, with illustrations.

Again, there are so many. Here are a few of my favorites:

*Sing!* by Joe Raposo (Henry Holt and Company 2013)
I was an old-school *Sesame Street* child, and I loved this song. When it came out in book format I was so excited, but it's hard to sing!! (It spans an entire octave.) However, the beauty of this book is it tells you "Don't worry that it's not good enough, for anyone else to hear, just sing, sing a song." Therefore, singing it off key makes it even more special!

*I Love You Too* by Ziggy Marley (Akashic Books 2014)
This book has such sweet illustrations and text. I like to read/sing this and then play the song and dance.

*Here We Go Round the Mulberry Bush*, contributors Sophie Fatus and Fred Penner (Barefoot 2007)
This is a great multicultural version of this song. It is fun to talk about how kids in other countries do things.

Along with song and rhythmic books, I should also add that I use flannels the same way. Although flannel boards with a variety of flannel pieces are old and low-tech, they remain popular in storytimes. A great example of this is Flannel Friday's Blog. They have many

Photo 4.1  Here are some pictures of "This Is the Way We Brush Our Teeth."

Photo 4.2  I love this picture of Alice showing off her teeth.

Photo 4.3  Here is Ruth doing a magnet version of *Lady with the Alligator Purse* by Nadine Bernard Westcott (Joy Street Books, Little Brown & Co. 1988). Ruth loves this song, and I was happy to see her make the images from the book so we could do it in our storytimes. In the book the images are somewhat small.

examples of popular, present-day flannels, and they have a great Facebook page as well (http://flannelfridaystorytime.blogspot.com). I do a flannel that is a song and play it on the guitar, or I sing with the story as I do the flannel, or I do a rhythmic flannel. For an example of a song, we have a cute flannel of a tree, a big sun, and kids playing underneath it. I put that up and we sing "Mr. Sun" (a song by Raffi). I do the same with "Ladybug Picnic" (from *Sesame Street*: https://www.youtube.com/watch?v=vX9J7WcYtxI). This song also works great for counting. We count the 12 ladybugs as we put them on the flannel board, and then we sing the song and dance. Other great examples are "Five Green and Speckled Frogs" and "Five Coyotes," sung by Nancy Stewart (http://www.nancymusic.com/Coyotes.htm).

For an example of a rhythmic flannel, I like "One, Two, Buckle My Shoe" (a popular English nursery rhyme). No song to sing, but a great example of a steady rhythm.

## Incorporating Instruments

I do this three ways: (1) I play an instrument, (2) I bring in children to play instruments, and (3) I let the children play with instruments.

A.   Do not be intimidated. Find an instrument you like and use it! I talked to a sweet woman at a conference who played flute in high school. After seeing my session, she went and bought a flute and is now using it in her storytimes! Can you imagine how cool it would be to hear the "Alphabet Song" on a flute? If you do not have an instrument, talk to your administration about purchasing one. You can get a relatively nice ukulele for $100, and with YouTube, you can learn easily! We have brought in autoharps, dulcimers, Native American pan flutes, electric pianos, and drums. In fact, a drum is a great first instrument for educators, because you can beat out the rhythm of a book or mimic rhythm.

Photo 4.4  Here are Alice and I talking about rhythm on a drum.

Another thing that works well is talking about how instruments are different and the same and also pointing out shapes, loud/soft, fast/slow, and so on.

Photo 4.5  Here we compare the guitar to the drum. "They both have circles, and the sound comes out of the circles."

Then Alice plays the drum and we copy the rhythm she plays.

Photo 4.6  We call this "Rhythm with Alice." Sometimes I drum on my guitar, but usually I clap with the caregivers.

B.   Find a child who plays an instrument and ask him or her to be a guest presenter. Kids love to see other kids perform. I find they love it and are inspired much more than when an adult plays an instrument. For example, when I first started my afternoon storytimes by myself, I showed videos of people playing instruments. I would always pick an expert musician that played fabulously, but what I noticed was that kids love the videos of kids playing, of course! I started looking for kids that played instruments and were willing to play for storytime. It was easier than I thought! I announced at my storytimes that I was looking for kids that played instruments or talked to music teachers. Most children and their parents are excited to do this. They get to perform to a group of their peers, and you get to give your storytime children a real experience of an instrument played by another child! It is a win-win situation!

I use *What in the World Is a Violin?* by Mary Elizabeth Salzman (ABDO 2012) This is a great series of books that talk about many instruments. As I am reading, I have the girls point out what the book is talking about, using their instruments.

I have the kids showing the scroll, neck, bridge, and strings. I do not go into too much detail, due to the young age of my kids in storytime.

Photo 4.7  Here the kids are showing their violins. We talk about the different sizes and the basic parts of the instruments.

I also compare the violin to my guitar. It's great for talking about big, little, even small, medium, and large!

Photo 4.8  Here they are playing a basic melody and a scale.

I have them start with a simple song the storytime kids know, like the "Twinkle Twinkle Little Star." The kids asked if they could play a more complicated piece, which I was happy to have them do, and then we all played together and the kids danced!

Photo 4.9  We be jammin'!

C.    Let the kids play instruments, and allow the kids to touch the actual instruments. Children must experience an instrument on their own. Krissy, our early literacy expert, has done a fabulous job of purchasing/making a variety of instruments such as purchased wooden percussion frogs, small rainmakers, and emptied and cleaned honey bear containers filled with beans.

Photo 4.10  Here is a little girl with a shaker, while her baby brother has some wrist bells. (Yes, they are in his mouth, but he is experiencing an instrument!)

During Toddler Time, I usually have a music interlude, where we hand out shakers and then play to a song that I play either on the guitar or on our iPad. I do like to interact with the kids and pattern how to use the shakers, so playing a song on the iPad works best. This works well with toddlers, because they get the shaker, but also have to give them back and it is a nice break/segue time between activities.

For musical storytimes, because we have two people, I play guitar and Ruth or Alice pattern the instrument. With the bigger groups, we always wait to hand out instruments until the end. I have listed some of the songs we use in Chapter 5, "Themed Storytime and Scripts."

One more thing about letting the kids play instruments: I feel it is *very important* to let the children play the instrument that I play. This could be because I have heard so many stories about adults that have instruments but never let kids touch them. I remember being at a harp concert, and there were eight *beautiful* harps on stage. It was a kids' concert, so there were many children in the audience. I watched a small child inch closer and closer to the stage and then jump up and rush to touch one of the harps. He was quickly stopped and started crying. But I thought, why not, at the end, let that child come back and touch the instrument? What was once a fascination with something so beautiful (the instrument and the music) became a negative event. This is why, at the end of every musical storytime, I always take the time to let the children experience the guitar or whatever instrument we have played. Yes, we have broken a drum or two, and my guitar has some bumps and scratches. Nevertheless, I have had so many fabulous interactions with babies and children of all ages touching, strumming, throwing the pick in the guitar, drumming on the body of the guitar, feeling the vibration on the guitar when I play the strings, and I could go on. Sometimes, it is the first experience the child has ever had with an instrument, and like I have said before, it is magical!

Ruby is one of my regulars. She has been attending since she was a baby with her older sister who has since aged out, but here, Ruby is asking me to play the chords to a song. I try to play the chords and let them strum.

Photo 4.11  Here are some pictures of the kids playing. I let them use either their fingers or the guitar pick. Most of the time they use the pick, since it makes more noise.

Photo 4.12  Ruby in her Valentine storytime pajamas.

Here is one of my favorite Ruby stories: when we asked the kids what they wanted to do when we were singing "I'm in the Mood" (a song by Raffi), she said, "Slide down a rainbow!" Now, try doing that with a guitar in your hand.

Photo 4.13  We are so lucky to create these connections with children. Say cheese!

## Presenting with a Partner

Disclaimer: In this section, I do not want to discourage *anyone* from not doing a musical storytime because they are on their own. I did musically based storytimes by myself for quite a while, and they worked just fine, and I still do Toddler Times by myself and play the guitar every week. Like I said at the beginning, if I can convince you to even just play an instrument during your storytime, I have gotten my point across, but I also want to be truthful as to what has worked best for our library in presenting a musical storytime—plus give you some convincing arguments you can present to your administration.

As much as I would like to say that I am a great storyteller, I am *nothing* without the material and especially my coworkers. I am always looking for new books, and I take inspiration from the people I work with. I cannot stress enough how creating and presenting these storytimes with two people make it so much more manageable and way more fun. Did I say incorporating instruments was a way to make it fun? Sometimes, and maybe I should say a *lot* of times, I get laughing so hard because of something Alice and/or Ruth says or does that I have to stop and catch my breath.

The second person makes musical storytime so much easier on multiple levels. I know in our limited work field, it is hard to find the time and money for two staff to do storytime. Nevertheless, I have four main points to argue the necessities of doing musical storytimes with two people (even if that second person is a volunteer): (1) you have a second pair of hands, (2) it saves the storyteller's voice and is not as stressful, (3) collaboration creates a better work environment, and (4) it helps with crowd management and safety.

(1)   *A second pair of hands.* Two is truly better than one!

Photo 4.14  Here are Ruth and I doing "Oh Hey, Oh Hi, Hello" (Jim Gill).

Photo 4.15  Here we are doing "Name of My Frog" (Bryant Oden).

Notice Ruth following the words with her fingers, thus leaving me able to play the song. Ruth is patterning Print Awareness!

Alice and I used to do "Name of My Frog" (song by Bryant Oden) with puppets, but it goes so fast, and there are 18 animals! So we made pictures. I could *never* do this song by myself. The pictures really make the song more interesting. So here you see Ruth going through all the pictures of the animals, and again I can sing and play.

(2)   *A second voice to protect yours.* Taking turns doing stories is invaluable to ensure you both stay strong and can support each other when needed. Alice is constantly drinking water, and when I am reading, she always has her trusty water bottle on hand. If I am not feeling 100 percent, Alice does more stories and vice versa. It is such a win-win.

(3)   *Opportunity to collaborate.* Doing musical storytimes together has brought us closer as a team. My stress load is lighter, because of not having to do a 45-minute storytime by myself, and we learn from each other. If we forget anything or need to prep for something, that second person can be so helpful to assure your storytime's success and avoid burnout.

I have had caregivers tell me countless times, "The reason you are so successful is because you can tell that you love what you do." If I had to do two musical storytimes a week by myself, it would be hard to emit that love!

This brings up the fourth point about having a second person at musical storytimes with large groups.

Photo 4.16  Ruth and I are always laughing at each other.

Photo 4.17  Ruth is modeling silly behavior, while I play "Silly Dance Contest" by Jim Gill. Yes, Ruth can be *very* silly.

(4)  *Crowd management and safety.* Having a second person makes it much easier to handle large groups. When Alice and I started, we averaged 80 people at these storytimes, we quickly outgrew our regular story space, and we can get loud. We moved the storytimes to our auditorium, which holds up to 230 people. It worked great, but it was a large space and we not only needed two people for the storytime, we also had a volunteer to manage stroller parking. We started averaging 100-plus people!

Once we moved to the new storytime space, after the remodel in 2014, things became a little bit easier because musical storytimes were in the Children's Library, which is not as isolated as the auditorium. But safety is always an issue working with children. One time, Ruth and I were right in the middle of storytime, and a very excited (possibly drunk) woman came in and started dancing and singing. She started engaging with kids she did not know. I kept playing while Ruth put down her ukulele and went over to the lady and kindly asked if she could talk to her outside of the story space. Ruth explained that the storytime was for caregivers and their kids. The lady understood and left. People hardly noticed the incident. If I had been by myself, I would have had to stop the storytime to ask her to leave.

To sum up, the three main things I do to create a musical storytime are:

1.  Choose books or flannels with a built-in rhythm or melody.
2.  Play an instrument and let the kids play instruments.
3.  Have two storytellers to present the program.

These are core for me to present a great storytime that I love doing, and the kids learn and have fun too!

Next, I will talk about why music is important to make early literacy fun and how using the Six Practices and Five Skills makes it easy and, of course, fun!

# WHY MUSIC IS IMPORTANT IN EARLY LITERACY

"I would teach children music, physics, and philosophy; but most importantly music, for the patterns in music and all the arts are the keys to learning."

—Plato

There are countless articles about the importance of music in our lives. Why is music especially important for kids? According to an article from Bright Horizons Family Solutions (2010), "a 2016 study at the University of Southern California's Brain and Creativity Institute found that musical experiences in childhood can actually accelerate brain development, particularly in the areas of language acquisition and reading skills. According to the National Association of Music Merchants Foundation (NAMM Foundation), learning to play an instrument can improve mathematical learning and even increase SAT scores." This fabulously succinct article goes on to explain the stages of child development and how music enhances the brain. It reminds us that music helps the body and mind work together, "Music ignites all areas of child development and skills for school readiness: intellectual, social and emotional, motor, language, and overall literacy."

We have a distinct advantage because we are working with very young children and those little brains that are developing so quickly!

According to another article by Kids Music Corner (n.d.), from the United Kingdom, "[When children's brains are developing.] Children's brains are like sponges that soak up anything that's going. That means children are much more ready to hear new things than adults. Many adults think that certain types of music (for example, heavy classical music) are not for children. In fact the opposite is often true. If an adult has not heard a particular type of music in childhood, then they will not normally like that music as an adult. This means they will ignore it. On the other hand, a child will just take in new music as yet another new experience in their lives."

This article shows the importance of implementing all styles of music into a child's learning and that, really, as educators, we have no limits to what we can teach musically.

As early literacy educators, we should use music as an ally. It should not be daunting. Do not worry if you cannot sing or have never played an instrument. I have seen storytellers that have a hard time singing, but they do sing. Why? Because they are being examples for the caregivers. Or they play recorded music, because it's what feels comfortable to them. And just think, if you can play a recorded song at storytime, why not get out a drum and play a rhythm to it? Or get out rhythm sticks and let everyone tap out a rhythm to the music. This can only make our storytimes stronger and give caregivers simple powerful skills that they can pass on to their children. And, as is shown in these articles, those skills can only ignite and expand a child's knowledge.

One last example of the power of music as an integral part of children's education is the non-profit educational organization Guitars in the Classroom. This organization trains teachers to implement music into any curriculum to enhance learning: any subject and all age ranges, from preschool to high school. According to their website, 75 percent of the teachers that enroll in this program have no prior musical training. The key is a guitar in the classroom and a collaborative curriculum (between teachers and their students) that incorporates songwriting and making music. "Music can help teachers be far more effective in conveying information, building classroom community, and differentiating instruction so it fits the needs of individual students" (Guitars in the Classroom, n.d.).

Their success stories are vast and inspiring! Research highlights from a 2009 assessment showed improved student engagement and increased confidence and motivation to learn.

This style of learning bridges a gap between English and non-English-speaking students, and 75 percent of kids that follow the curriculum say they want to continue playing an instrument (Guitars in the Classroom, n.d.).

I have already mentioned ECRR 1 and 2 earlier in this chapter. In stressing the importance of music in children's lives, I would like to discuss ECRR 2, or the Five Practices (Play, Read, Sing, Talk, and Write). It is easy. When introducing a musical instrument in a storytime, a piano, for example, we will READ books about pianos, fiction and nonfiction. Then I will bring up YouTube and show different types of music being played on the piano; we TALK about the different styles of playing (jazz, classical, rock and roll, etc.) We also discuss different shapes of a piano. Next I bring out an actual piano. (You can get a keyboard relatively cheap or even ask for donations.)

Then I play a simple scale and TALK about the different keys and what they are called. We WRITE A–G in the air as I show/play them the key. Then we SING "Twinkle Twinkle Little Star," or some other simple song I can play easily on the keyboard. At the end, I always let them PLAY with the instrument. I feel this is crucial in cultivating the child's curiosity and creating a connection with the instrument. I hear all the time, "We have a guitar at home, but my child isn't allowed to play it." In a teaching situation, such as we are providing, we must be hands-on, and that counts for instruments too.

When you think about everything I've described so far, you really have a ready-made storytime! Moreover, it is so fun.

Here are specific (and my favorite) ways to use the Five Practices and the Six Skills:

# FIVE PRACTICES

## Play

- Pretend you're an animal moving to music. How would each animal move? You can stress the rhythm of the music and how each animal would beat out the rhythm.
- "Silly Dance Contest" (song by Jim Gill). We have adapted this song to cover themes like safari animals. "Dance like a monkey if you want to . . ."
- Going to the moon. This is a great way to incorporate imaginative play into storytime. There is an example of this in Episode 4 of *Read with Us*, at 9:50 (https://boulderlibrary .org/youth/read-with-us/). In the show, we do not use music, but in storytime, I like to do this to the song "Space Oddity" (song by David Bowie). I got this idea from my daughter, who loved this song when she was three. We would always count down in the song, and she would yell, "Blast off!!" And then we would pretend to go to the moon.

## Read

- Post words and sing out the syllables. The music can be different (fast, slow), but that rhythm of the word stays the same.

- The simple act of playing an instrument while you're reading will make a book come alive.
- "List of Dances" (song by Jim Gill). He actually posts only the dances, "Tall, small, hop, stop, and so on" to read and thus dance. We post the words and a picture of a child doing the motion. We have an example of that in our televised program, *Read with Us*, Episode 3 (https://boulderlibrary.org/youth/read-with-us/).

# Sing

- Most nursery rhymes are easy to play on an instrument. Sometimes I will sing the "Alphabet Song"; then I get the guitar out and have everyone join in singing with me. Anecdote: I had a very mellow group once for Toddler Time, and when we started singing the alphabet song, every child went into their caregiver's lap and sat quietly while we all sang to them. I thought most of them would fall asleep. It was so sweet!
- Sing a book.
- Call and respond songs and/or books: Alice made up this to go with *I Went Walking* by Sue Williams (Harcourt Brace 1989):

  (Sung to the tune, Frère Jacques)
  Storyteller: "I went walking."
  Group: "I went walking."
  Storyteller: "What did you see?"
  Group: "What did you see?"
  Storyteller: "I saw a green duck."
  Group: "I saw a green duck."
  Storyteller: "Looking at me."
  Group: "Looking at me."
  And so on.

# Talk

- Dialogic reading with a book is obvious. Dialogic means to ask questions about what is going on in the text, and you encourage talk when you ask kids about the books you read in storytime, but you can also talk about the instrument you are using, even if it's a simple shaker. How is the sound made? What is inside the shaker? This is important because it gets the child thinking about how the instrument is made and how it works. I like using text-to-self comparisons because it heightens the child's understanding of said instrument. A child will tell me that the instrument is quiet, and I respond, "Can you be quiet like the guitar? Can we be loud?"
- Along with talking about the instrument, at the end I always try to take time and talk to every child who wants to touch and play the guitar. One girl *loved* the guitar, and she would ask me questions about how the strings stayed on the guitar, why it has a hole, how do the tuning pegs work, and so on. She took those questions to her caregiver, who in turn ended up buying her a ukulele. She would play off and on, and finally her mom started her in lessons. She is now eight and can play the

ukulele very well! Her mom says it has helped her self-esteem, and she has even played with me at storytime!

# Write

- Dance with scarves and have them move specifically. (Make a square, circle, or the letter "A.")
- Drum and have them draw a shape in the air to the beat.
- I love to do "The Shapes Songs" by A. J. Jenkins. I play and sing it very slowly and have the kids and caregivers trace the shapes in the air with their fingers as we sing the song.

# SIX SKILLS

1.  *Narrative Skills*

    - Telling a story playing an instrument. For example, *Gunnywolf* by A. Delany (Harper & Row 1988). You can incorporate the Alphabet Song easily.
    - Playing any song with a beginning, middle, and end ("Itsy Bitsy Spider," "Twinkle Twinkle Little Star," etc.).
    - Telling a story which incorporates any instruments you are using. For example, *Sing Sophie* by Dayle Ann Dodds (Candlewick Press 1997). Sophie plays the guitar through the whole story. And solves the problem at the end too!

2.  *Print Awareness:*

    - Displaying song lyrics so the caregivers can sing along. (We do this a lot.)
    - Singing the alphabet songs and then finding letters. I will display specific letters or even the whole alphabet if I have time to put them all out. We also look for letters on shirts or on a book.
    - Singing the shapes song and then finding shapes. I do this the same as with the alphabet; I will display shapes, but I also really give this some time and let the kids find them. I am always amazed what children will find. One storytime we had a hard time finding stars. I had a child come up to me after the storytime and show me the bottom of her shoe. Sure enough, there were stars on the soles of her shoes!!

3.  *Print Motivation*

    - Singing any song that reinforces love of the library or love of books. I wrote this to the tune of "Take Me Out to the Ballgame" (by Edward Meeker):

      Oh how I love to be reading
      Oh how I love my books
      Short ones and long ones and pop-ups too
      There are so many it's hard to choose

Photo 4.18 Here is a picture of Ruth and me doing "The Name of My Frog" (song by Bryant Oden). Ruth is literally pointing out the print!

> How I love to go to storytime
> When I can't go it's a shame
> I read one, two, three books at night, then I read all day!

- Retelling a beloved story on the guitar. We will read a book version of "Twinkle Twinkle Little Star" and then play it (or vice versa).
- Using an instrument while you are reading a story. Alice loves *Tacky the Penguin* by Helen Lester (HMH Books 1988). While she is reading it, I will lightly strum as background music and use the guitar to accent parts of the story. I love sliding down a guitar string to make the sound of Tacky and his friends diving in the water.

4. *Letter Knowledge*

- Singing any alphabet song and then finding letters. (See "Print Awareness.")
- Singing any shapes song and then finding shapes and also drawing them in the air. (See "Print Awareness.") I love this song Krissy made up, and it is easy to play on the guitar:

  (To the tune of *Sesame Street*'s "C is for Cookie")
  B is for Baby, it's a letter don't you see?
  B is for Baby it's a letter don't you see?
  B is for Baby, it's a letter don't you see?
  Baby, Baby, Baby starts with B.

- Sing "The Phonics Song" by A. J. Jenkins. I found this on KidsTV123, but I adjusted it to the alphabet signs we have. It is long, but the parents will help singing. I have done this for Toddler Time several times and always think I will have to cut it short, but it goes just fine.

Photo 4.19  Here Ruth and I are just singing! (and Ruby is in her heart pajamas jumping).

5.  *Vocabulary*

- What I love about vocabulary and using an instrument is you are not tied to the exact song as played on a recording. You can increase the amount of words you use by singing songs and asking for suggestions and improvising, like in "The Colors Song" and also "The Phonics Song."
- Play "The Colors Song" (by A. J. Jenkins. https://www.youtube.com/watch?v= xPWZu4LDmQM) (or any song that talks about colors), and then ask, "What other colors do we see?" Funny story: Once when I was doing this in storytime I asked for pink. Surprisingly enough, none of the children had pink on. Until a young girl raised up her skirt to show off her beautiful new pink underwear, stating, "I have pink on!!"
- "The Phonics Song" (by A. J. Jenkins. https://www.youtube.com/watch?v=saF3-f0XWAY). Any song that lists words with the alphabet will work. Then I do a few letters, especially if I know the names of the children. "What other words start with "A"? Alice!"
- "The Name of My Frog" (song by Bryant Oden). I do love this song and use it a lot. The song has more than 20 animals!
- "Silly Dance Contest" (song by Jim Gill) or "I'm in the Mood for Singing" (song by Raffi), using new ways to move.

6.  *Phonological Awareness (my favorite!!)*

- Incorporate an instrument and show how it can sound loud and soft, you can play it fast and slow, and so on.
- Clap with song or story. This can be tricky when you have your caregivers join in because they will naturally speed you up. Do not hesitate to stop and slow them down.
- Drum with a song or story. We do this a lot. You can also use rhythm sticks.
- Drum, clap, or even jump to the syllables, not just the rhythm. Kids love to do this with their name.
- Dance and explore movement with the rhythm of the words or just the music. This is where the guitar works well, because you can control the speed of the song. But this also works well singing a capella (without an instrument). You can dance like an animal or as a specific shape or emotion!
- Listen to a song and help kids hear a specific instrument, such as the drum or bass guitar. This works best with older kids. I have them listen for and then clap to the drumbeat. But I have been surprised by younger kids who can pick out a drum and piano too.

## Summing Up

In my years of doing storytimes, I am constantly amazed at the power of music and learning. I believe using music makes the ECRR early literacy tips come alive for children. Jim Henson said, "[Kids] don't remember what you try to teach them. They remember what you are."

I have children that are now in high school that come to me at the library and remember my stories, my songs, and that I played the guitar. Do they remember that exact moment they realized "Twinkle Twinkle Little Star" was written text? Or when they came up with a new way to dance? No, but the connection between literature and music stuck. They are reading, and hopefully, learning to find what they love to do in this world.

Jim Henson also said, "Music is an essential part of everything we do. Like puppetry, music has an abstract quality which speaks to a worldwide audience in a wonderful way that nourishes the soul." This quote speaks to me wholeheartedly! I have children in my storytime that speak other languages and many that are just developing those words to communicate. Music and rhythm are something they all are drawn to from day one. From the beating of their mother's heart, to the rhythms they hear every day, to the songs that fill their souls. It is nourishment—and essential for me and my passion for early literacy.

## ALBUMS AND SONGS

Bowie, David. *Best of Bowie.* Parlophone. Remastered Ed. 2002. "Space Oddity."
Gill, Jim. *Jim Gill Makes It Noisy in Boise, Idaho.* Jim Gill Music. 1995. "Oh Hey, Oh Hi, Hello" and "List of Dances."
Gill, Jim. *Jim Gill Sings the Sneezing Song and Other Contagious Tunes.* Jim Gill Music. 1993. "Silly Dance Contest."
Jones, Howard. *Dream into Action.* WEA/Elektra. "Things Can Only Get Better."
Oden, Bryant. *The Songdrops Collection. Vol. 3.* Songdrops Music. 2013. "The Name of My Frog."
Raffi. *Rise and Shine.* Rounder Records, 1996. "I'm in the Mood."
Raffi. *Singable Songs for the Very Young: Great with a Peanut-Butter Sandwich.* Rounder Records. 2007. "Mr. Sun."

## PICTURE BOOKS USED AS SONGS

Fatus, Sophie, and Fred Penner. *Here We Go Round the Mulberry Bush.* Bath: Barefoot, 2007.
Guthrie, Woody. *This Land Is Your Land.* New York: Little Brown and Company Hachette Book Group, 1998.
Guthrie, Woody, and Vladimir Radunsky. *Bling Blang.* Cambridge, MA: Candlewick Press, 2000.
Marley, Ziggy. *I Love You Too.* Illustrated by Ag Jatkowska. Brooklyn, NY: Akashic Books, April, 2014.
Miller, J. Phillip. *We All Sing with the Same Voice.* New York: HarperCollins Children's Books, 1982.
Raposo, Joe, and Tom Lichtenheld. *Sing: Sing a Song.* New York: Christy Ottaviano Books, Henry Holt and Company, 2016.
Westcott, Nadine Bernard. *The Lady with the Alligator Purse.* New York: Little, Brown and Company, Inc., 2003.

# BOOKS

Delaney, A. *The Gunnywolf.* New York: Harper & Row, 1988.

Dodds, Dayle Ann, and Roseanne Litzinger. *Sing, Sophie!* Cambridge, MA: Candlewick Press, 1997.

Fatus, Sophie, and Fred Penner. *Here We Go Round the Mulberry Bush.* Bath: Barefoot, 2007.

Guthrie, Woody. *This Land Is Your Land.* New York: Little Brown and Company Hachette Book Group, 1998.

Guthrie, Woody, and Vladimir Radunsky. *Bling Blang.* Cambridge, MA: Candlewick Press, 2000.

Lester, Helen. *Tacky the Penguin.* New York: Houghton Mifflin Company, 1988.

Marley, Ziggy. *I Love You Too.* Illustrated by Ag Jatkowska. Brooklyn, NY: Akashic Books, April, 2014.

Miller, J. Phillip. *We All Sing with the Same Voice.* New York: HarperCollins Children's Books, 1982.

Perkins, Al. *Hand, Hand, Fingers, Thumb.* New York: Random House, 1969.

Raposo, Joe, and Tom Lichtenheld. *Sing: Sing a Song.* New York: Christy Ottaviano Books, Henry Holt and Company, 2016.

Salzmann, Mary Elizabeth. *What in the World Is a Violin?* Minneapolis, MN: ABDO, 2012.

Scheer, Julian. *Rain Makes Applesauce.* New York: Holiday House, 1964.

Schofield-Morrison, Connie, and Frank Morrison. *I Got the Rhythm.* New York: Bloomsbury, 2014.

Westcott, Nadine Bernard. *The Lady with the Alligator Purse.* New York: Little, Brown and Company, Inc., 2003.

# WEBSITES

Bright Horizons Family Solutions. "Children and Music: Benefits of Music in Child Development." https://www.brighthorizons.com/family-resources/e-family-news/2010-music-and-children-rhythm-meets-child-development (accessed June 2017).

Every Child Ready to Read. http://everychildreadytoread.org/about/ (accessed December 2017).

Guitars in the Classroom Research Page. www.guitarsintheclassroom.org/learn-about-us/research/ (accessed August 2017).

"The Importance of Storytelling." www.hslda.org/Contests/Essay/2013/Cat3/Carpenter.pdf (accessed December 2017).

Kids Music Corner. "Why Is Music Important?" http://kidsmusiccorner.co.uk/why-is-music-important/ (accessed March 2017).

# Chapter 5

# Themed Storytimes and Scripts

This chapter is full of scripts from our various storytimes, during which we use instruments and music.

## MUSICAL STORYTIMES WITH RUTH AND MELANIE

We always have gotten requests for an afternoon storytime, but that is such a tricky time. We have tried reading clubs during the summer and craft times, but they have never been very successful. We did a survey, and it overwhelmingly asked for another musical storytime. I started doing a 4:00 P.M. storytime by myself, but quickly became overwhelmed. I was doing Toddler Time in the morning and then musical storytime in the late afternoon. So my boss gave me the okay to bring on a second person, like we do with our morning musical storytime. We hired Ruth!! She and I alternate Toddler Times and we do the afternoon musical storytime together.

Ruth came on board with a ukulele and a ton of enthusiasm. I was very excited to have another person to play an instrument. We go back and forth playing songs or accompanying a book. The library just purchased a banjo-ukulele, which is so fun to play with books, and it is much louder, so when we play together, the guitar doesn't dominate, as it does with a ukulele. Ruth is great with props and flannels. Together we also do a Dance Party, which is simply all songs, movement, and props. Next I share some of the scripts from some of our favorite musical storytimes. We always start with the same song: "I'm in the Mood" by Raffi. Note: these scripts are ambitious; we always go into a storytime having more material than we actually use. We always let the children tell us where to go, sometimes cutting something short or sometimes letting it run longer. We always do a relatively strict 45-minute storytime.

# Food: Fruits and Veggies

**Intro song on guitar and ukulele**: "I'm in the Mood" by Raffi

Let kids decide what movement, but segue into eating, gardening, and so on.

**Fingerplay:** "Five Little Peas"

Five little peas in a pea pod pressed. (Keep hands together and fingers down.)
One grew, two grew and so did all the rest (Put up one finger, two fingers, and the rest.)
They grew . . . and grew . . . and did not stop (Open hands wide.)
Until one day the pod went POP! (And CLAP!)

(Repeat fingerplay)

**Book:** Call and respond: *Today Is Monday* by Eric Carle

**Book:** *Rain Makes Applesauce* by Julian Scheer

I have everyone clap a slow rhythm and ask them to repeat, "Rain makes applesauce." Ruth says, "Oh you're just talking silly talk."

**Imaginative play:** Have kids pretend they are an apple seed. (Let them lead.)

Prompts, "How does a seed grow?" Hopefully they will respond, "With water and sun." We roll in a ball (the seed) and as the rain come and sun shines, we grow and grow till we stand tall and then reach our arms out like branches, then our fingers open as blossoms. The apples grow heavy and drop off the end of our hands. Now we can make applesauce! We pick up the apples, mash them up, and have yummy applesauce!

**Song on guitar:** "Apples and Bananas" by Raffi

**Flannel:** "I've Lost My Banana," adapted from "Frère Jacques"

Flannels are house shapes of different colors. We have two flannel bananas hidden behind the various houses. We sing (as a call and respond):

I've lost my banana
Respond (I've lost my banana.)
Where can it be?
(Where can it be?)
Maybe it is hiding.
(Maybe it is hiding.)
Look and see.
(Look and see.)

Ask the children for a color and search till you find the first banana. Sing the song again to find the second.

**Song/Movement:** "Banana Dance"

Form the banana, form, form the banana. (Bring your right arm up as you say this.)
Form the banana, form, form the banana. (Bring your left arm up.)
Peel the banana, peel, peel the banana. (Bring your right arm down.)
Peel the banana, peel, peel the banana. (Bring your left arm down.)
Go bananas, go, go bananas. (Jump around and act crazy!)
Go bananas, go, go bananas.
(Oh yeah, you repeat that!!)

There are many examples of this song with plenty of verses online.

**Book:** *Jamberry* by Bruce Degen

Or Flannel, from JBRARY, which is a big canoe and five large images of fruit:

Over the bridge (Put arms over head.)
And under the dam (Sweep arms down.)
Looking for berries, berries for jam (Hand above, eyes searching.)
One berry, two berries, pick me a BLUEBERRY! (Pretend to pick the berries and eat
   them up!)
(Continue with other fruit: strawberry, raspberry, blackberry, and cherry.)

**Flannel:** A-P-P-L-E (Ruth modified this version adapted from "Bingo was his name-o")

Flannel of an apple with the letters above it. We put the printed song, "There was a fruit
so round and sweet and apple was its name-o" on the flannel board so the caregivers will
help sing:

There was a fruit so round and sweet and apple was its name-o, A-P-P-L-E, A-P-P-
L-E, A-P-P-L-E and apple was its name-o

At this point, pick a favorite puppet to jump out from behind the flannel board.

| Melanie: | "Pig!! What are you doing here?" |
| Pig (Ruth): | "I'm hungry." |
| | *Pig eats the letter E.* |
| Melanie: | "Pig!! You ate the letter E. How are we going to sing the song?" |
| | *Pig continues to eat the letter.* |
| Melanie: | "I guess we will have to clap where the letter used to be, do you think we can do that?" |

And so on.

**Embarrassing side story:** The first time Ruth and I did this, she was voraciously having
the pig eat the letters and was really getting into it. I reacted horrified every time the pig

took a letter, but when the pig took the letter "P," Ruth yelled, "Pig!! You took a P!" I burst out laughing and got the giggles at the thought of the pig "taking a pee." I couldn't get it back. I laughed the whole rest of the flannel. I'm sure my face was bright red from trying not to giggle. Now every time we do this flannel, Ruth looks at me and very slowly says, "Look Miss Melanie, the pig is *eating* the letter P." I start cracking up anyway. (I'm such a child.) It's one of my very favorite flannels.

**Segue:** "We can put our berries and apples on some shortbread and it will be so yummy!"

**Song, on ukulele, with dancing:** "Shortnin' Bread"

Ruth plays and Melanie patterns dancing.

**Ending song on guitar:** "If You're Happy and You Know It"

But we change it to eating food or picking apples, whatever. "If you're happy and you know it eat a cherry, and so on." And then segue into "If you're happy and you know it say goodbye."

Melanie plays and Ruth patterns. (And then we collapse!!)

## Food: Pizza and Ice Cream

Since we do a healthy foods theme, we had to throw in pizza and ice cream!

**Intro song on guitar and ukulele:** "I'm in the Mood" by Raffi

Let the kids decide what movement, but segue into eating pizza and ice cream.

**Hello song:** "Peanut Butter Jelly" (adapted from Bread and Butter, on JBRARY: https://www.youtube.com/watch?v=Tx61o23Vvns)

(Rhythm is to clap hands and slap thighs.)
Peanut butter, jelly, marmalade, and jam, let's say hello as quiet as we can, "Hello" (whispering).
Start rhythm again:
Peanut butter, jelly, marmalade, and jam, let's say hello as loudly as we can, "Hello" (yelling).

Many variations, such as:

Fast and slow
Serious and silly
Happy and sad

**Book:** *Knick Knack Paddy Whack* by Barefoot Books

This is a great multicultural version that uses instruments and ends at a pizza place.

**Song, on guitar, call and respond:** "I Am a Pizza" by Charlotte Diamond

**Book, with actual drum pounding a rhythm:** *Groovy Joe: Ice Cream and Dinosaurs* by Eric Litwin

(Oh Eric, I do love you, but I miss your Pete the Cat skills.) This book works well when you have everyone sing, "Love my doggy ice cream, love my doggy ice cream!" And also when they say with you the main refrain of the book, "It's awesome to share."

**Flannel:** "We all Scream for Ice Cream"

This is a simple flannel we use for counting and colors. It's simply 20 scoops of ice cream (different colors/flavors) and some cones.

You have everyone say, "I scream, you scream, we all scream for ice cream."

Then count the amount of scoops you put on the cone. Depending on your group, you can count by two, add and subtract, or whatever.

**Book:** *Today Is Monday* by Eric Carle

**Ending song:** "Twist and Shout" by The Beatles

# Love, Peacefulness, and Emotions

**Intro song on guitar and ukulele:** "I'm in the Mood" by Raffi

Let kids decide what movement, but segue into hugging, kissing, and so on.

**Book:** *The Peace Book* by Todd Parr

Ruth sings this. She just makes up a tune.

**Song on guitar and ukulele:** "Peace Like a River" by Elizabeth Mitchell

This is a great sing along. It's easy, and our caregivers love it.

**Segue:** But sometimes I don't feel peaceful; I have many emotions, I feel sad. Can you show me sad? (Kids make a sad face.) Can you show me happy? and so on, but end with mad.

**Book/Song:** *If You're Angry and You Know It* by Cecily Kaiser

This book works very well for dialogic reading. It displays a situation that makes a character angry, but on the next page it shows skills to handle your anger like "walk away, take deep breaths, bang a drum." I love it. It's a little didactic, but it works. It's done to the tune, "If You're Happy and You Know It."

**Book/Song on ukulele:** *I Love You! A Bushel and a Peck* by Frank Loesser

**Song/Movement:** "Skinnamarink" (based on the JBRARY version: https://www.youtube .com/watch?v=Ix_LyeuYbcI)

**Song/Sign language:** "Love Grows" (based on the version sung by Miss Nina)

**Book/Song:** *We All Sing with the Same Voice* by J. Phillip Miller

**Book/Song on guitar:** *What a Wonderful World* by George David Weiss and Bob Thiele

**Embarrassing side story:** I always cry reading this book. Also the book *We All Sing with the Same Voice*, so after doing both of these, I could barely get through the end of this story. Thank goodness Ruth was there too. I hear the lyrics, and I look at all those beautiful young children I'm reading to . . . I'm tearing up just thinking about it!!

**Ending song and bubbles:** "Three Little Birds" by Bob Marley

We played this on our iPad, since Ruth and I were both desperately trying to blow enough bubbles for everyone.

## Pollinators

We were asked to do a special storytime since Boulder was celebrating Pollinator Appreciation Month. Ruth dressed up like a bee, and I (gulp) dressed up like a flower. Pollinator Appreciation Month is September, but this could also work as a great Spring-themed storytime.

**Intro song on guitar and ukulele:** "I'm in the Mood" by Raffi

Let kids decide what movement, but segue into buzzing, crawling, and flying . . . like our favorite insects!!

**Book:** *Up, Down, and Around* by Katherine Ayres (sung to the tune of "Twinkle Twinkle Little Star")

**Book/Song:** *Inch by Inch* by David Mallett

**Flannel/Song on guitar:** "Ladybug's Picnic" based on the *Sesame Street* version by Bud Luckey and Donald Hadley (https://www.youtube.com/watch?v=vX9J7WcYtxI)

We have 12 Ladybugs, and Ruth puts them on the flannel board as I count with the song. This is long, and the lyrics are quick, but it worked. But, it made me feel old; not one of my caregivers knew this song from *Sesame Street*!

**Book:** *Giant Pop-Out Bugs: A Pop-Out Surprise Book* by Amelia Powers

We have the entire series of the Pop-Out Surprise Books and I *love* them, but they are out of print. We use them a lot in our Read with Us shows. Get them if you can!!

**Song:** "Bumblebee, (Buzz Buzz)" by The Laurie Berkner Band

**Book:** *Ants Go Marching* by Childplay

We marched around the room as we sang this. It's long, so accommodate as needed.

**Song on guitar:** "Thank You Honey Bee" by Jeff and Paige (https://www.youtube.com/watch?v=LzXaI5J8bDI)

We shortened this, but it worked! And the honeybee dance is so fun. We sang it twice.

# READ WITH US: FILMED STORYTIMES

After the success of our musical storytimes, we started getting a lot of requests for examples of what we were doing in the storytimes. One of my goals to accommodate those requests was to start a blog. I wanted to pattern it after JBRARY and highlight those things we did in storytime. After researching many librarians' blogs, I quickly decided against it. There were so many, and I just didn't feel young and hip enough. Ironically enough, we had Channel 8, our local television station, ask us if we would be willing to film some of our storytimes. Walla! A perfect way to document some of the things we had been doing in our storytimes! We began filming in 2016.

We discovered two main issues with filming storytimes: (1) finding materials and making sure we have permission for use from the performer and/or publisher and (2) filming storytimes and finding an audience.

The first issue, finding materials and making sure we have permission for use from the performer and/or publisher—lucky for us, we had an enthusiastic employee, Alyx Campbell, who was getting her MLS and totally willing to contact publishing companies for copyright permission regarding books. She would send Alice and me lists of books sorted by publisher and then send a request for use. For an example of this, I have a template I received from Andrea Cleland. She helps film StoryBlocks for the Colorado Libraries for Early Education (https://www.storyblocks.org/). (I would love to give a shout-out to Andrea Cleland. She is a kids' yoga teacher and has incorporated that love of yoga into her storytimes at the Clearview Library District in Colorado. She is a perfect example of doing what you love and incorporating it into early literacy.)

This template has been adjusted to our libraries' request for permission of use:

What we found was that companies were mainly concerned if we were going to be using their book for profit; we had to add in the line about there being "no charge to the public."

Date

Hello _____, (add a contact or name here or "To whom it may concern")

We have been asked to record a storytime show for our municipal television broadcasting station, Boulder Channel 8 (https://bouldercolorado.gov/channel8). A fellow librarian and I would read books while being filmed, showing the books to a small, live studio audience. If allowed, we would announce the title and author before reading, and we would also like to include close-up shots of the pages of the books. We would be very grateful if we could use your books!

Starting sometime in 2016, Boulder Channel 8 will air each storytime show on a Sunday and then periodically throughout the following week. It will also be available to watch online on our library website: https://boulderlibrary.org/ and on Channel 8's website: https://bouldercolorado.gov/channel8.

The storytime show will also be syndicated to other municipal Channel 8s in surrounding towns. There is absolutely no charge to the public and they will be able to watch it on TV or online for free.

We appreciate your time and consideration.
Sincerely,

Melanie Borski-Howard
Youth Services Specialist
Boulder Public Library

We received great responses from smaller publishing companies like Gecko Press and no response from the larger, like Hyperion. But Alice and I worked with the books we had permission to use. I learned a lot through this process. As librarians we are spoiled to be able to use any books and songs we want for our storytimes. Alice and I had to meet and really discuss how we could group the books we did have and move from books to flannels to rhymes, and so on.

The second issue: filming storytimes and finding an audience. We wanted this to be a real storytime experience, so of course, we needed families. But also, I hesitated bringing in kids that were under two, because I felt that was contradictory to the controversial discussion regarding no screen time for babies. Abundant articles such as "More Screen Time Linked to Lower Psychological Ability" published by the American Pediatric Society in 2010 really made me rethink what we wanted this storytime to accomplish. In fact, the whole storytime felt contradictory to what a library storytime is all about.

What I came back to was the heart of storytime: the children and their connection to literature and promoting early literacy. I felt, regardless of age, if we are capturing the true storytime experience, for better or worse, we would be doing our job. When choosing families, I always seek out those children from my most engaged storytimes. But a huge component is that the caregiver is also engaged and actively participating.

The following are four of our *Read with Us* storytime scripts. You can access the filmed versions here: https://boulderlibrary.org/youth/read-with-us/.

# Read with Us #1

Taping session: February 16, 2016

Song: "Oh Hey, Oh Hi Hello" (Jim Gill)
Book: *Moo!* by David LaRochelle (Walker Books: Bloomsbury)
Book: *Giant Pop-Out Farm* (Chronicle)
Activity: Sequencing—recall order of things on the farm
Song: "Old MacDonald" (traditional)
Song: "Mary Had a Little Lamb" (traditional)
Book: *Mary Had a Little Lamp* by Jack Lechner/Bob Staake (Bloomsbury)
Activity: Rhyming exercise—examples from book
Book: *You Can Do It Too!* by Karen Baicker (Handprint Books)
Activity: Drum echo
Book: *I Got the Rhythm* by Connie Schofield-Morrison (Bloomsbury)
Song/Dance: "Silly Dance Contest" (Jim Gill)

All copyrighted works used by permission.

Bloomsbury Press: *Moo!* by David LaRochelle
*Mary Had a Little Lamp* by Jack Lechner
Chronicle Books: *Giant Pop-Out Farm*
Jim Gill: http://www.jimgill.com/
"Oh Hey, Oh Hi Hello"
"Silly Dance Contest"

# Read with Us #2

Taping session: March 22, 2016

Song: "Everybody Wave Hello" by Margie La Bella
Book: *Lola at the Library* by Anna McQuinn (Charlesbridge)
Song: "Twinkle, Twinkle Little Star" (traditional)
Activity: Writing—draw shapes in the air. End with circle.
Book: *Plaidypus Lost* by Janet Stevens (Holiday House)
Song: "Where, Oh Where" (traditional)
Book: *Anton Can Do Magic* by Ole Könnecke (Gecko Press)

Book: *Giant Pop-Out Pets* (Chronicle Books)
Song: "The Name of My Frog" by Bryant Oden
Song /Dance: "Rhythm in the Scarves" by Johnette Downing

*Unfortunate side story: This song worked fabulously because it is fun and looks great on the screen with the scarves flying everywhere. We got permission once, and I e-mailed Johnette and asked her if we could use her song in another episode. Unfortunately, we had neglected checking on the actual show and found that Channel 8 had cited the song incorrectly. Johnette did not give us permission to use the song a second time. We learned an important lesson! Always check that your sources and citations are correct.*

All copyrighted works used by permission.

Bryant Oden: "The Name of My Frog," http://www.songdrops.com/
Charlesbridge: *Lola at the Library* by Anna McQuinn, illustrated by Rosalind Beardshaw
Chronicle Books: *Giant Pop-Out Pets*
Gecko Press: *Anton Can Do Magic* by Ole Könnecke
Holiday House: *Plaidypus Lost* by Janet Stevens and Susan Stevens Crummel
Johnette Downing: "Rhythm in the Scarves," Wiggle Worm Records ASCAP (gratis synchronization license), http://johnettedowning.com/
Margie La Bella: "Everybody Wave Hello," http://www.musictherapytunes.com/wp/

## Read with Us #3

Taping session: April 19, 2016

Song: "Hello, Friends" ("Frère Jacques": traditional)
Book: *Babies Can't Eat Kimchee!* by Nancy Patz
Activity: "Pat-a-Cake, Pat-a-Cake" (traditional)
Book: *Giant Pop-Out Food* (Chronicle Books)
Activity/Flannel: Ice Cream Cones
Song: "A-P-P-L-E" ("B-I-N-G-O": traditional)
Book: *First the Egg* by Laura Vaccaro Seeger
Book: *Bedtime for Mommy* by Amy Krouse Rosenthal
Song/Flannel: "Five in the Bed" (traditional)
Book: *A Bed for Kitty* by Yasmine Surovec
Book: *Hush Little Baby* by Sylvia Long
Song/Dance: "List of Dances" by Jim Gill
Song: "The Sneezing Song" by Jim Gill
Song/Dance: "Silly Dance Contest" by Jim Gill
Song: "Goodbye, Friends" ("Frère Jacques": traditional)

Copyrighted works used by permission.

Bloomsbury Press: *Babies Can't Eat Kimchee!* by Nancy Patz
*Bedtime for Mommy* by Amy Krouse Rosenthal
Chronicle Books: *Giant Pop-Out Food*
*Hush Little Baby* by Sylvia Long
Jim Gill: http://www.jimgill.com/
"List of Dances"
"The Sneezing Song"
"Silly Dance Contest"
*First the Egg*, 2007 by Laura Vaccaro Seeger. Reprinted by permission of Roaring Brook Press, a division of Holtzbrinck Publishing Holdings Limited Partnership All Rights Reserved.
*A Bed for Kitty*, 2014 by Yasmine Surovec. Reprinted by permission of Roaring Brook Press, a division of Holtzbrinck Publishing Holdings Limited Partnership All Rights Reserved.

## *Read with Us #4*

Taping session: May 18, 2016

Song: "Hello Everybody" by Mary Sue and Cari
Book: *Lola Loves Stories* by Anna McQuinn
Book: *Zoom Rocket Zoom!* by Margaret Mayo
Activity: Countdown and pretend spacewalk
Book: *Un-Brella* by Scott E. Franson
Book: *Snow* by Uri Shulevitz
Book: *Supertruck* by Stephen Savage
Activity: Pretend play
Song: "Oh Where, Oh Where" (traditional)
Activity: Drum echo
Song: "My Body's an Instrument" by Mary Sue and Cari

*Side story: I know Mary Sue. She actually works at the library when she isn't on tour with her group Strangebyrds. She has done storytimes with me and is super sweet. This song got partially cut due to the length of the show. We had to make sure to do it a second time in its entirety.*

Song/Dance: "The Sit Down, Stand Up Song" by Rick Goldin

Copyrighted works used by permission.

Bloomsbury Press: *Zoom, Rocket, Zoom!* by Margaret Mayo
Charlesbridge Press: *Lola Loves Stories* by Anna McQuinn
Mary Sue and Cari:

from Music with Kids, 2000, re-released 2009

"Hello Everybody"

"My Body's an Instrument"

Rick Goldin: http://www.rickgoldin.com/

"The Sit Down, Stand Up Song"

*Snow*, 1998 by Uri Shulevitz. Reprinted by permission of Roaring Brook Press, a division of Holtzbrinck Publishing Holdings Limited Partnership All Rights Reserved.

*Supertruck*, 2015 by Stephen Savage. Reprinted by permission of Roaring Brook Press, a division of Holtzbrinck Publishing Holdings Limited Partnership All Rights Reserved.

*Un-Brella*, 2007 by Scott E. Franson. Reprinted by permission of Roaring Brook Press, a division of Holtzbrinck Publishing Holdings Limited Partnership All Rights Reserved.

# TODDLER TIMES SPECIFIC TO THE SIX SKILLS

Kristina (Krissy) Jensen, our early literacy specialist, introduced Caregiver Storytimes to the Boulder Public Library in 2008. We called them "Caregiver" Storytimes because they were (and still are) aimed at educating the caregivers during that vital time for a child's brain development from zero to three years. Krissy designed the programs following the Every Child Ready to Read (ECRR) curriculum:

> The Public Library Association (PLA) and Association for Library Service to Children (ALSC) concluded that public libraries could have an even greater impact on early literacy through an approach that focused on educating parents and caregivers. If the primary adults in a child's life can learn more about the importance of early literacy and how to nurture pre-reading skills at home, the effect of library efforts can be multiplied many times.
>
> Teaching parents and other caregivers how to support the early literacy development of their children is the basis of ECRR @ your library. When the first edition of ECRR was introduced in 2004, the focus on educating parents and caregivers was a significantly different approach for many libraries; one that certainly has proven its value. (http://www.everychildreadytoread.org/about)

This was a very different approach for me. I certainly had noticed the difference between a preschool storytime, when you are just reading to a group of children, and a library storytime, where the children are (usually) with their caregivers. That caregiver element creates a very different atmosphere for the children. At my regular storytimes, I am reading to the caregivers too, and I always throw in a title, like Mike Reiss's book, *The Boy Who Looked Like Lincoln* (Price Stern Sloan 2003), or even better, Mem Fox's *Harriet You'll Drive Me Wild* (Harcourt Brace 2000), because I know they appeal to the caregivers. Both books have elements that only an adult would understand. But what Krissy was doing was different. I wasn't just reading books for the caregivers to listen to; I was actually giving the caregivers tools that they could use at home with their children.

During my training, Krissy showed me all the scripts she had designed and told me to make them my own. I really appreciated that. Her scripts were vast. We ended up with three sets: Baby Time (0–12 months), Wobblers and Walkers (12–24 months), and Toddler Time (24–36 months). All three had specific scripts to the Six Skills—18 scripts in total. Along with the scripts she also put together a two-page list of rhymes that we hand out to the caregivers so they can reference (and participate in) what we are doing.

The main thing I remember from my training was, "Slow down, Melanie, keep your voice quieter. Slow down . . . Melanie, slow down!" It really took a lot for me to curb that theatrical background as a storyteller and realize that I was teaching these children language. It was one of the best things I could have learned as a storyteller.

Here is one of the original scripts:

**Toddler Time Script (Style 1)**

**Phonological Awareness**

CD: *Quiet Time* (by Raffi)

1.  Introduction
2.  Program Discussion

    a.  Rhymes, songs, book sharing, play
    b.  Child's comfort
    c.  Today's emphasis: phonological awareness
    d.  Interact with your child (eye contact, touch, talk)

3.  Activities

    a.  Hello song: "Hello, Baby"
    b.  Moderate song: "Itsy, Bitsy Spider"
    c.  Moderate activity: "Five Little Monkeys"
    d.  Low activity rhyme: "This Is My Father"
    e.  Lullaby: "Lavender's Blue"
    f.  Transition to book sharing: "Open Them, Shut Them"
    g.  Book sharing

    1.  *I Went Walking* (SPC Williams) ["SPC Williams" is the location code on where to find the title in our library]
    2.  *Sheep in a Jeep* (SPC Shaw) [what rhymes with sheep? Car? Jeep? Etc.]
    3.  *Jazz Baby* (SPC Wheeler)
    4.  *Five Little Monkeys Jumping on the Bed* (SPC Christelow)
    5.  *Goodnight, Moon* (SPC Brown)

    h.  Low activity rhyme: "Pease Porridge Hot"
    i.  Low activity song: "Where Is Thumbkin?"
    j.  Moderate activity rhyme: "Ten Little Fingers"
    k.  Book with instruments: "Shake Shake Shake" (SPC Pinkney)
    l.  Goodbye song: "If You're Happy and You Know It" [make some noise]

6.    Adult/child interaction with books
7.    Resume music; free play with baby toys; informal discussion

We hand out this sheet to the caregivers so they can follow along to the script.

**Toddler Time Rhymes**

**Phonological Awareness**

**Toddler Time, Boulder Public Library**

**Hello, Baby**

*Tune: "Frère Jacques"*

Hello, (Name), Hello, (Name),
How are you? How are you?
You make us so happy,
You make us so happy.
Yes, you do . . .
Yes, you do . . .

**Itsy Bitsy Spider**

***This Is My Father***

This is my father,
This is my mother,
This is my brother, tall;
This is my sister,
This is the baby.
Oh! How I love them all.

***Lavender's Blue***

Lavender's blue, dilly, dilly,
Lavender's green.
Close your dear eyes, dilly dilly,
And have sweet dreams.

***Open Them, Shut Them***

Open them, shut them,
Give a little clap.
Open them, shut them,
Put them in your lap.

## Pease Porridge Hot

Pease porridge hot,
Pease porridge cold,
Pease porridge in the pot,
Nine days old.
Some like it hot,
Some like it cold.
Some like it in the pot,
Nine days old.

## Where Is Thumbkin?

*Tune: "Frère Jacques"*

Where is Thumbkin,
Where is Thumbkin?
Here I am,
Here I am.
How are you today, sir?
Very well, I thank you.
Run and hide,
Run and hide.

## I Have Ten Little Fingers

I have ten little fingers,
And they all belong to me.
I can make them do things,
Would you like to see?

I can shut them up tight,
Or open them wide,
I can put them together,
Or make them all hide.

I can put them up high
Or put them down low,
I can fold them quietly,
And hold them just so.

## If You're Happy and You Know It

If you're happy and you know it clap your hands.
If you're happy and you know it clap your hands.

If you're happy and you know it and you really want to show it.
If you're happy and you know it clap your hands.

If you're happy and you know it wave goodbye.
If you're happy and you know it wave goodbye.
If you're happy and you know it and you really want to show it.
If you're happy and you know it wave goodbye.

## Phonological Awareness (Style 2)

I love the scripts Krissy made. And they work great for someone just learning how to do Toddler Times, but what I particularly love about Krissy's training is that she let me be me. Here is a script I made from what I learned:

**Introduction:** The topic (Phonological Awareness) Who I am, introduce Pat (my volunteer assistant)

**Hello Song** (as listed in the original Toddler Time Rhymes): Hello Toddler, clapping to the rhythm (repeat) and then again to the syllables (repeat)

**Fingerplays:**

Itsy Bitsy Spider (as listed in the original Toddler Time Rhymes) (repeat)
Wheels on the Bus
Where is Thumbkin (as listed in the original Toddler Time Rhymes) (repeat)

**Book:** *I Got the Rhythm* by Connie Schofield-Morrison

Have caregivers repeat the senses, Blink Blink, Sniff Sniff, and so on.

Introduce drum and a slow beat. Make it faster than slow. (I have my volunteer do this, so I can read the book.)

**Book:** *Hand, Hand, Fingers, Thumb* by Al Perkins to a drum beat; caregivers can clap.

**Movement:** "Here We Go Up" (sung to "Here We Go Looby Loo")

Caregiver can lift child, stand up, and crouch down or lift arms up and down.

(Start crouching on the ground.)

Here we go up up up (standing up)
Here we go down down down (crouch back down)
Here we go up up up (standing up)
Here we go down down down (crouch back down)

Repeat.

**Book with visuals:** *Music Man* by Debra Potter

Have pictures of the actual instruments in books taped up all around. Sing the book and then find the instrument and pretend to play it. (My volunteer helps the kids find the pictures.)

**Activity:** Freeze play. Get out real instruments and let the kids all pick one. Use "Go" and "Stop" signs to indicate playing and stopping. Gather instruments if they become too big of a distraction.

Introduce electric piano. Play "The Alphabet Song" and have them sing along. Talk about tempo and how the tempo can be fast and slow. Play "The Alphabet Song again," fast and then slow. Then put on a song and dance! Fast and then slow.

**Goodbye Song:** "If You're Happy and You Know It" (from the original list of rhymes)

Incorporate what we learned, if you're happy and you know it bang a drum, play the xylophone, blink your eyes, and so on.

As I have said before, at the end of this storytime it is important to let the kids play with the piano and drum and all the other instruments during play time after storytime.

# MUSICAL STORYTIME WITH ALICE AND MELANIE

I won't go into the history of these storytimes, since I have already discussed it in the beginning. But, retrieving scripts for this book has been tricky. When Alice and I started these storytimes, we would come together with books we wanted to do and go back and forth reading them. We literally just improvised fingerplays in between, or we would throw in puppets with the books that we were doing. But once I started incorporating the guitar and our numbers became increasingly bigger, we started meeting once a week to put together scripts. I have put some of those scripts next. But remember, it can be that easy to go script-free! Just pull together a bunch of musical books you like doing and maybe some fun movements and flannels and just go! Let the children lead and have fun!!

# Zoo and Ocean Animals

**Opening Song:** "When Cows Wake Up in the Morning" (with Zoo or Ocean Animal puppets)

**Book:** *Somewhere in the Ocean* by Jan Ward

Lead in imaginative play: have the kids get ready to go deep sea diving. Ask them what they need to go diving way under the water.

**Funny Note:** The kids usually go along with this quite well, bathing suit, wetsuit, goggles, breathing mask, air tank, goggles, but I once a had a little girl say, "Most important is our beautiful seashell necklace!" so we went deep sea diving with our beautiful necklaces on!

**Song/Flannel:** "There's a Hole in the Bottom of the Sea" by Danny Kaye

**Movement:** "The Jellyfish Song." This is based on Tooty Ta. Alice learned this at camp, but we have never been able to find the person who originated it. It is so much fun! The kids love it! You can also find an example of this on *Read with Us*, Second Season, Episode 1 (https://boulderlibrary.org/youth/read-with-us/).

**Sit back down/transition song:** "Head, Shoulders, Knees, and Toes"

**Book/Song:** *Seals on the Bus* by Lenny Hort

**Book/Song:** (played on guitar) *Going to the Zoo* by Tom Paxton

**Ending Song:** "Sleeping Bunnies" by Russ (adapted to zoo and or ocean animals)

This has become a *beloved* song and probably the most requested song we get for a musical storytime. The kids lying on the ground and waking up to hop is adorable. We adjust it to whatever theme we are presenting, and I also take requests. We have been unicorns, stormtroopers, even carrots. I asked the child what motion we do when we are carrots, and he started running his fists down his chest and belly and said, "We peel the carrot!"

# Emotions and Being Silly

**Opening Song:** "Clap your Hands" based on the version by Margie La Bella (https://www.youtube.com/watch?v=VHya0irmbB4)

**Book:** *Plaidypus Lost* by Janet Steven (Have the kids draw a circle when you say, "this story goes around and round.")

**Song played on guitar:** "Shapes Song" based on the version by A. J. Jenkins (https://www.youtube.com/watch?v=IkZs2_1-YJU)

Alice draws the shapes on the whiteboard and has the caregivers and kids draw the shape in the air with their fingers.

Go back to *Plaidypus Lost* and talk about all the emotions the girl goes through in the books: happy, scared, worried, sad.

**Book:** *Little Bunny Foo Foo: Told by the Good Fairy* by Paul Brett Johnson

Talk about the good fairy and what emotion she is feeling (anger).

**Book/Song:** *If You're Angry and You Know It* by Cecily Kaiser (definitely act this out)

**Book/Song:** *If You're Happy and You Know It* by James Warhola (act out too—be silly!)

"What is one of our favorite emotions? Being silly!"

**Book, played on guitar:** "Down by the Bay" by Raffi

**Movement:** "Swimming Swimming, in a Swimming Pool." Based on the version by Miss Nina's Weekly Video Show (https://www.youtube.com/watch?v=Fxk4ZQPv1YE)

**Book/Song:** *Lady with the Alligator Purse* by Nadine Bernard Westcott

**Ending song:** "Rhythm in the Scarves" by Johnette Downing

Hand out scarves and dance.

# Pets, Animals, and Grandmas (Yes, Grandmas)

We do this theme in the summer or around a holiday when we know we'll have some grandmas in the audience.

**Hello song on guitar:** "Hello Everybody" (song by Mari Sue and Cari)

**Book/Song:** *This Old Van* by Kim Norman

**Movement:** Three Bears Cha! Cha! Cha! Based on the chant by the Zoomers. (You watch this on ZOOM Season Three Episode 27: https://www.youtube.com/watch?v=ncA9rIFlNYQ)

**Book/Song:** *Ten Little Puppies* by Alma Flor Ada and Isabel Campoy (Don't forget to count down from 10 with this book. It works great!)

**Song:** "Name of My Frog" by Bryant Oden

**Book and movement:** *Croaky Pokey* by Ethan Long (Alice printed out a large fly and tied it to a string on a stick; we all try to grab it while we are doing a "croaky" pokey.)

**Handheld with the guitar:** "There Was an Old Lady That Swallowed a Fly." We have pictures of all the animals the old lady eats. I sing/play the song, and Alice pretends like she is the old lady and acts it out. The kids love to watch her "eat" everything.

**Book:** *The Nuts: Sing and Dance in Your Polka Dot Pants* by Eric Litwin

**Polka dot pants dance:** Pass out polka dots (dot stickers) and have everyone put them on their pants. Play the song "Polka Dot Pants Dance": www.thenutfamily.com/videos.html.

# Bodies and Food

**The opening song:** "Hello Hello Hello" by Lorri Ada

This was written by one of our storytime caregivers! She also is part of our audience on *Read with Us.* Her song is on Episode 8, a capella, using simple sign language, and also Episode 10, with the guitar (https://boulderlibrary.orgu/youth/read-with-us/). Lori used to be a preschool teacher and came up with this simple, sweet song. We are so happy to use it!

Hello Hello Hello
Hello Hello Hello
We're happy that you're here today, hello hello hello.

We're going to read some books
We're going to read some books
We're happy that you're here today. We're going to read some books

(You can make up additional lyrics:)
We're going to sing some songs
We're going to clap our hands.
And so on.

**Book:** *Please Baby Please* by Spike Lee (Alice makes up a tune to go with this.)

**Book:** *I Am a Baby* Kathryn Madeline Allen (I sing this to the tune, "I Am a Pizza" by Charlotte Diamond)

**Rhythm with Alice:** playing a rhythm on the drum. Drum a beat and have audience repeat by clapping.

**Book:** *I Got the Rhythm* by Connie Schofield-Morrison

**Movement:** "Head, Shoulders, Knees, and Toes." Regular, fast, and slow.

**Book/Song:** *Knick Knack Paddy Whack*, Barefoot Books edition

**Imaginative play:** Make a pizza: get the pretend dough, roll it out, and ask the kids what they want on the pizza. It is very important that you let the kids lead. It always ends up that you put gross stuff on the pizza. (I have had dirt, ice cream, yogurt, lollipops, etc.) Then you cook the pizza in a pretend oven for 10 seconds, slice the pizza, and eat it! Make sure to make your best disgusted tasting face!

**Song on guitar:** "I Am a Pizza" by Charlotte Diamond

"Are you still hungry?"

**Movement:** Form the Banana. We improvise and ask the kids for other foods. It's hilarious coming up with things to do with the food, squeeze the orange, dip the carrot sticks, mash and drink the grapes, and so on.

"Now that we have eaten, it's time to take a nap!"

**Ending song on guitar:** "Sleeping Bunnies" by Russ

# SENSORY STORYTIMES

We had Douglas County Libraries present how they do Sensory Enhanced Storytimes at one of our staff meetings. It was inspiring! At Boulder Public Library, we have a Sensory-Friendly Concert Series, which has been very successful. We thought a natural addition would be to start a storytime catered to children living on the autism spectrum. We contacted the founder of BrainSong, a group of parents devoted to expanding the world of the arts to all children, especially those with special needs. Just going to the BrainSong website, I was amazed at how the love of music was pivotal to these children's learning success. From the website:

> Did you realize that music is the oldest form of communication? Or just how profound music can be on the brain's development and abilities? World renowned neurologist Oliver Sacks has spent much of his life denoting this fact (see his book *Musicophilia*); an entire lab at MIT is now researching the incredible effect music has on our body's largest muscle. Researchers have shown that in Alzheimer's patients, when they are in their last stages of the debilitating disease, and can no longer recognize themselves in the mirror, they can still hear an old, familiar tune, stand up and sing! And when we hear music, we use more of our brain energy than during any other task in life.
>
> So, it makes sense that we, as caregivers, would turn to music to help our children with Autism fight for a better today and tomorrow.

We also worked with the Association for Community Living to get further support and funding, along with our own Boulder Public Library Foundation, to help us start up this storytime.

We work from a template, so the scripts do not deviate and are somewhat repetitious. We Storyboard each activity so kids and parents know what is coming. The Storyboard consists of icons representing each thing we are going to do in the storytime (Welcome Song, Book, Song, Fingerplay, Scarves, Flannel Board, Closing Song, Bubbles). We use a lot of music.

Here are two of our scripts:

**Script #1. Theme: Bears and Colors**

**Welcome song:** "The More We Get Together"

> The more we get together
> Together, together
> The more we get together
> The happier we'll be
> 'Cause your friends are my friends
> And my friends are your friends
> The more we get together
> The happier we'll be

**Book:** *Bear Sees Colors* by Karma Wilson

**Song with parachute:** "These Are the Colors Over You" (Tune: "Twinkle, Twinkle Little Star")

Red and green and yellow and blue
These are the colors over you.
Red like an apple and green like a tree
Yellow like the sun and blue like the sea.
Red and green and yellow and blue
These are the colors over you.

*Repeat.*

**Fingerplay:** "Bear Is Sleeping" (Tune: "Frère Jacques")

Bear is sleeping, bear is sleeping (lay head on hands)
Wake him up, wake him up (make peek-a-boo motion with hands)
Come and say hello bear, come and say hello bear (wave hello)
Time to eat, time to eat (grab food and put in mouth)

*Repeat.*

**Book:** *Brown Bear Brown Bear* by Bill Martin

**Scarves**

**Song:** "Put Your Scarf on Your Head" (Tune: "If You're Happy and You Know It")

Put your scarf on your head, on your head.
Put your scarf on your head, on your head.
Put your scarf on your head, on your head, on your head.
Put your scarf on your head, on your head.

Other suggested lyrics:

Put your scarf on your belly, on your belly . . .
Wave your scarf in the air
Throw your scarf in the air
And so on.

**Flannel Board:** *We're Going on a Bear Hunt*

Based on the book by Michael Rosen.

**Closing song:** "If You're Happy and You Know It Say Goodbye"

**Bubbles**! **Song:** "Waltzing with Bears" (song by Priscilla Herdman)

**Script #2. Theme: Trains**

**Welcome Song:** "The More We Get Together"

The more we get together
Together, together
The more we get together
The happier we'll be
'Cause your friends are my friends
And my friends are your friends
The more we get together
The happier we'll be.

**Book:** *Freight Train* by Donald Crews

**Song:** "Down by the Station" (tune is similar to "Alouette")

Down by the station, early in the morning
See the little choo-choo trains, all in a row
See the engine driver pull his little handle
Puff puff! Ding ding! And off we go!

**Fingerplay:** "This Little Train"

This little train ran up the track (run fingers up arm if possible, or in the air)
It went "toot toot!" (beep nose or pretend to ring bell in air)
And then it came back! (run fingers back the other way or back down arm)
This little train ran up the track (run fingers up other arm or in other direction)
It went "toot toot!" (same beeping or ringing motion as before)
And then it came back! (run fingers in the other direction or down arm)

**Book:** *I Love Trains!* by Philemon Sturges

**Scarves:** "The Wheels on the Train" (use scarves to exaggerate motion)

The wheels on the train go clickety-clack, clickety-clack, clickety-clack
The wheels on the train go clickety-clack, on the railroad tracks

Other verses:

The engine on the train goes chug, chug, chug . . .
The conductor on the train says "Tickets please" . . .
The people on the train go bounce, bounce, bounce . . .
The whistle on the train goes toot, toot, toot . . .

(As few or as many verses as the kids and families want)

**Flannel board:** "Clickety-Clack"

(Four flannels of a train: the Engine, Coal Car, Box Car, and Tank Car)

Clickety-clack, clickety-clack,
Here comes the train on the railroad track!
Clickety-clunn, clickety-clunn,
Here comes ENGINE number one.
Clickety-clew, clickety-clew,
Here comes COAL CAR number two.
Clickety-clee, clickety-clee,
Here comes BOX CAR number three.
Clickety-clore, clickety-clore,
Here comes TANK CAR number four.
Clickety-cloose, clickety-cloose
Here comes the last—it's the caboose!

**Closing Song:** "If You're Happy and You Know It Say Goodbye"

**Bubbles! Song:** "New River Train" by Raffi

# ALBUMS AND SONGS

Beatles, The. *Please Please Me.* Parlophone. 1963. "Twist and Shout."
Diamond, Charlotte. *10 Carrot Diamond.* Hug Bug Records. 1985. "I Am a Pizza."
Downing, Johnette. *The Second Line—Scarf Activity Songs.* Johnette Downing. 2003. "Rhythm of the Scarves."
Gill, Jim. *Jim Gill Makes It Noisy in Boise,* Idaho. Jim Gill Music. 1995. "Oh Hey, Oh Hi, Hello" and "List of Dances."
Gill, Jim. *Jim Gill Sings the Sneezing Song and Other Contagious Tunes.* Jim Gill Music. 1993. "The Sneezing Song" and "Silly Dance Contest."
Goldin, Rick. *I Like to Read.* CD Baby. 2012. "Sit Down, Stand Up."
Herdman, Priscilla. *Star Dreamer; Nightsongs & Lullabies.* ALACAZAM! 1988. "Waltzing with Bears."
Kagen, Jeff. *Songs from the Trail.* Jeff Kagen Conscious Rock Records. 2009. "Thank You Honeybee."
Kaye, Danny. *There's a Hole in the Bottom of the Sea.* Fantastic Voyage. 2011.
La Bella, Margie. *Move!* Margie La Bella. 2009. "Everybody Wave Hello."
Laurie Berkner Band. The Best of the Laurie Berkner Band. Two Tomatoes Records. 2010. "Bumblebee (Buzz Buzz)."
Marley, Bob. *Exodus.* Island Records. 1977. "Three Little Birds."
Mitchell, Elizabeth. *You Are My Little Bird.* Smithsonian Folkways Recordings. 2006. "Peace Like a River."
Oden, Bryant. *The Songdrops Collection. Vol. 3.* Songdrops Music. 2013. "Name of My Frog."
Raffi. *More Singable Songs.* Rounder Records. 1987. "New River Train."

Raffi. *One Light One Sun*. Rounder Records. 1996. "Apples and Bananas."
Raffi. *Quiet Time.* Rounder Records. 2006.
Raffi. *Rise and Shine.* Rounder Records. 1996. "I'm in the Mood."
Raffi. *Singable Songs for the Very Young: Great with a Peanut-Butter Sandwich.* Rounder Records.
    2007. "Down by the Bay."
Rodgers, Mary Sue, and Minor, Cari. *Mary Sue & Cari, Music with Kids. Back Pocket Production.* 2007.
    "Hello Everybody" and "My Body's an Instrument."
Russ. *Sing & Play at School with Russ.* Claytunes Music. 2016. "Sleeping Bunnies."

# PICTURE BOOKS USED AS SONGS

Alma, Flora Ada, et al. *Ten Little Puppies*. New York: Rayo, 2011.
Carle, Eric. *Today Is Monday*. New York: Philomel Books, 1993.
Crisp, Dan. *Ants Go Marching*. Auburn, ME: Childs Play Intl. Ltd., 2008.
Engel, Christiane. *Knick Knack Paddy Whack*. Illustrated by Christiane Engel. Great Britain: Barefoot
    Books, Ltd.; United States: Barefoot Books, Inc., 2008.
Hort, Lenny. *Seals on the Bus*. New York: Henry Holt and Company, 2000.
Kaiser, Cecily, and Cary Pillo. *If You're Angry and You Know It!* New York: Scholastic, 2005.
Lechner, Jack, and Bob Staake. *Mary Had a Little Lamp*. New York: Bloomsbury Children's Books, 2008.
Loesser, Frank, and Rosemary Wells. *I Love You! A Bushel & a Peck: Taken from the Song, "A Bushel and
    a Peck."* New York: Harper Collins, 2005.
Long, Ethan. *Croaky Pokey*. New York: Holiday House, 2001.
Long, Sylvia. *Hush Little Baby*. San Francisco, CA: Chronicle Books, 1997.
Mallett, David, and Ora Eitan. *Inch by Inch: The Garden Song*. New York: HarperCollins, 1995.
Miller, J. Phillip. *We All Sing with the Same Voice*. New York: HarperCollins Children's Books, 1982.
Norman, Kim. *This Old Van*. New York: Sterling Children's Books, 2015.
Paxton, Tom, and Karen Schmidt. *Going to the Zoo*. New York: Morrow Junior Books, 1996.
Potter, Debra. "I Am the Music Man." Australian Child's Play, 2005.
Raffi and Westcott Nadine Bernard. *Down by the Bay*. New York: Crown Publishers, 1987.
Ward, Jan, et al. *Somewhere in the Ocean*. Flagstaff, AZ: Rising Moon, 2000.
Warhola, James. *If You're Happy and You Know It*. New York: Orchard Books, 2007.
Weiss, George, Bob Thiele, and Bryan Ashley. *What a Wonderful World*. New York: Atheneum Books
    for Young Readers, 1995.
Westcott, Nadine Bernard. *The Lady with the Alligator Purse.* New York: Little, Brown and Company,
    Inc., 2003.

# BOOKS

Allen, Kathryn Madeline, and Rebecca Gizicki. *I Am a Baby*. Chicago, IL: Albert Whitman & Company,
    2016.
Alma, Flora Ada, et al. *Ten Little Puppies*. New York: Rayo, 2011.
Ayres, Katherine, and Nadine Bernard. *Up, Down, and Around*. Cambridge, MA: Candlewick Press,
    2007.
Baicker, Karen. *You Can Do It Too!* Brooklyn, NY: Handprint Books, 2005.
Carle, Eric. *Today Is Monday*. New York: Philomel Books, 1993.
Chronicle. *Giant Pop-Out Farm*. San Francisco, CA: Chronicle Books, LLC, 2010.

Chronicle. *Giant Pop-Out Food.* San Francisco, CA: Chronicle Books, LLC, 2010.

Chronicle. *Giant Pop-Out Pets.* San Francisco, CA: Chronicle Cooks. LLC, 2010.

Crews, Donald. *Freight Train.* New York: Green Willow Books, 1978.

Crisp, Dan. *Ants Go Marching.* Auburn, ME: Childs Play Intl. Ltd., 2008.

Degan, Bruce. *Jamberry.* New York: Harper & Row, 1983.

Engel, Christiane. *Knick Knack Paddy Whack.* Illustrated by Christiane Engel. Great Britain: Barefoot Books, Ltd.; United States: Barefoot Books, Inc., 2008.

Fox, Mem, and Marla Frazee. *Harriet, You'll Drive Me Wild.* San Diego: Harcourt Brace, 2000.

Franson, Scott E. *Un-Brella.* New Milford, CT: Roaring Book Press, 2007.

Hort, Lenny. *Seals on the Bus.* New York: Henry Holt and Company, 2000.

Johnson, Paul Brett. *Little Bunny Foo Foo: Told and Sung by the Good Fairy.* New York: Scholastic Press, 2004.

Kaiser, Cecily, and Cary Pillo. *If You're Angry and You Know It!* New York: Scholastic, 2005.

Könnecke, Ole. *Anton Can Do Magic.* Minneapolis, MN: Gecko Press, 2010.

LaRochelle, David, and Mike Wohnoutka. *Moo!* New York: Walker Books for Young Readers, an Imprint of Bloomsbury, 2013.

Lee, Spike, and Tonya Lewis Lee. *Please, Baby, Please.* Illustrated by Kadir Nelson. New York: Simon & Schuster Books for Young Readers, 2002.

Litwin, Eric, and Tom Lichtenheld. *Groovy Joe: Ice Cream and Dinosaurs.* New York: Orchard Books, 2016.

Litwin, Eric, and Scott Magoon. *The Nuts: Sing and Dance in Your Polka Dot Pants.* New York: Little, Brown Books for Young Readers; Act Ina edition, 2015.

Loesser, Frank, and Rosemary Wells. *I Love You! A Bushel & a Peck: Taken from the Song, "A Bushel and a Peck."* New York: HarperCollins, 2005.

Long, Ethan. *Croaky Pokey.* New York: Holiday House, 2001.

Long, Sylvia. *Hush Little Baby.* San Francisco, CA: Chronicle Books, 1997.

Martin, Bill, Jr. *Brown Bear, Brown Bear.* New York: Henry Holt and Company, 1967.

Mayo, Margaret, and Alex Ayliffe. *Zoom, Rocket, Zoom!* New York: Walker Books for Young Readers, 2011.

McQuinn, Anna. *Lola at the Library.* Charlesbridge: Charlesbridge, 2006.

McQuinn, Anna. *Lola Loves Stories.* Illustrated by Rosalind Beardshaw. Watertown, MA: Charlesbridge, 2010.

Miller, J. Phillip. *We All Sing with the Same Voice.* New York: HarperCollins Children's Books, 1982.

Norman, Kim. *This Old Van.* New York: Sterling Children's Books, 2015.

Parr, Todd. *The Peace Book.* New York: Little, Brown and Company, 2004.

Patz, Nancy, and Susan L. Roth. *Babies Can't Eat Kimchee!* New York: Bloomsbury Children's Books, 2007.

Paxton, Tom, and Karen Schmidt. *Going to the Zoo.* New York: Morrow Junior Books, 1996.

Perkins, Al. *Hand, Hand, Fingers, Thumb.* New York: Random House, 1969.

Pinkney, Andrea Davis, and Brian Pinkney. *Shake Shake Shake.* New York: Red Wagon Books, 1997.

Potter, Debra. *I Am the Music Man.* Swindon, Australia: Child's Play. 2005.

Powers, Amelia. *Giant Pop-Out Bugs: A Pop-Out Surprise Book.* San Francisco: Chronicle Books, 2008.

Reiss, Mike, and David Catrow. *The Boy Who Looked Like Lincoln.* New York: Price Stern Sloan, 2003.

Rosen, Michael, and Helen Oxenbury (eds.). *We're Going on a Bear Hunt.* New York: Macmillan Publishing Company, 2005.

Rosenthal, Amy Krouse, and LeUyen Pham. *Bedtime for Mommy.* New York: Bloomsbury, 2010.

Savage, Stephen. *Supertruck.* New York: Roaring Book Press, 2015.

Scheer, Julian. *Rain Makes Applesauce.* New York: Holiday House, 1964.

Schofield-Morrison, Connie, and Frank Morrison. *I Got the Rhythm.* New York: Bloomsbury, 2014.

Seeger, Laura Vaccaro. *First the Egg.* New York: Roaring Brook Press, 2007.

Shaw, S.P.C. *Sheep in a Jeep.* Illustrated by Margot Apple. New York: Houghton Mifflin Company, 1986.

Shulevitz, Uri. *Snow.* New York: Farrar Straus Giroux, 1998.

Stevens, Janet, and Susan Stevens Crummel. *Plaidypus Lost*. New York: Holiday House, 2004.

Sturges, Philemon, and Shari Halpern. *I Love Trains!* Illustrated by Shari Halpern. New York: HarperCollins Publishers, 2001.

Surovec, Yasmine. *A Bed for Kitty*. New York: Roaring Brook Press, 2014.

Ward, Jan, et al. *Somewhere in the Ocean*. Flagstaff, AZ: Rising Moon, 2000.

Warhola, James. *If You're Happy and You Know It*. New York: Orchard Books, 2007.

Weiss, George, Bob Thiele, and Bryan Ashley. *What a Wonderful World*. New York: Atheneum Books for Young Readers, 1995.

Westcott, Nadine Bernard. *The Lady with the Alligator Purse*. New York: Little, Brown and Company, Inc., 2003.

Wheeler, Lisa, and R. Gregory Christie. *Jazz Baby*. Orlando, FL: Harcourt, 2007.

Williams, Sue. *I Went Walking*. Orlando, FL: Omnibus Books, Harcourt Inc., 1989.

Wilson, Karma. *Bear Sees Colors*. New York: Margaret K. McElderry Books, 2014.

# Chapter 6

# Outreach Storytimes

Wait a minute, don't you live at the library?

—A three-year-old I ran into at the grocery store

I have a learned a lot from doing library storytimes, but even more from my outreach to the community. Taking storytime on the road to kids, adults, and places you are unfamiliar with can prove to be challenging but necessary as a librarian/literacy coach. Getting the kids into the library is one thing, but going to them is something completely different. Finding the time, energy, and resources is hard but so worth it! Many times when I introduce the library to children, they have no idea about how a library operates. Or even that it is free to get a library card! It is integral to literacy to let people know what libraries have to offer. And doing storytimes is a great way to introduce young children to the library. In this chapter, I highlight what I have learned from going out of my comfort zone, the library. This was hard for me as a librarian/introvert. I like to be around books. And at first, I liked to know I had an arsenal of puppets, flannels, and so on. Everything I needed was in our office. It acted as a security blanket for me. But going out of my comfort zone really improved my confidence as a storyteller and made me appreciate my job as a librarian.

I have listed books that worked for me, but really, I try to stay on the cutting edge of new books for my outreach storytimes. Or at least follow the books and strategies other librarians are using. For this I find following the Storytime Underground Facebook group invaluable! (https://www.facebook.com/groups/storytimeunderground/)

## PRESCHOOL STORYTIMES

When my daughter attended preschool, we weren't making much money. We received tuition assistance, but I wanted to give back. I asked the owner if I could do storytimes; she didn't know who I was and did not respond until she found out I worked at the library. Not only did she let me start doing storytimes, but she traded my storytimes for my daughter's

Photo 6.1  I do love this purple guy!

full tuition! After my daughter left, they asked me to continue and hired me. I have been doing storytimes there now for 12 years!

For me, a preschool storytime is very different from a library storytime because there is no caregiver, so the books I choose are somewhat different. I still have the teachers in the room, but I find myself catering more to just the children. I have three main elements: (1) books (always the core of everything I do), (2) the guitar, and (3) my beloved sidekick: Larry.

I always bring books, but I alternate bringing the guitar and Larry. I open and close with the guitar and Larry. They *love* Larry, seriously. If you do not have a puppet sidekick, get one now! I use him occasionally for my regular storytimes at the library but not for musical storytimes.

I never have scripts for these storytimes. It's the same for my all-ages storytimes at the library. But I do always incorporate at least one new book and one book that highlights one of the ECRR's Five Practices: Play, Read, Sing, Talk, and Write. I always do all five practices, but I don't necessarily call them out. I always do imaginative play midway that corresponds with one of the books I have read. The lovely thing about preschool storytimes is that I get to read longer stories and can discuss what the story is about due to the smaller numbers of kids.

One of these storytimes (which runs about 30 minutes) could look like this:

**With Larry (who is hiding in my book bag)**
Me: "Guess who came with me today? Larry!!"

I get him out, and he waves to the kids, we sing some songs together, play peek-a-boo with the younger group, and so on. Then Larry goes into my bag and picks a super silly story that, of course, he smuggled in.

I read some books and always try to include imaginative play. For example, we read *Tree Is Nice* by Janice May Udry (HarperCollins 1984). I say, "Let's grow a tree! How do we do that?" And we go from there, planting a seed, giving it good dirt and water to grow, maybe with rain, maybe with a hose. If someone wants to grow an apple tree, we see the blossoms on the tree (I use my hand closed and then open it to represent a blossom), and then they grow into apples, and we pick them and make apple pie. Or, if a child wants to make a tree house in our tree, we get some (pretend) wood and build a tree house in our tree, and then it rains, so we get in our tree house to protect ourselves from the rain! (Both are actual scenarios that have happened during storytime.)

Then Larry yells from the book bag that's it time to go. He brings out one more book and we read it, then we sing a goodbye song together, and he gives everyone fist bumps and high-fives.

## With My Guitar

We open with a song, usually a movement song like "I'm in the Mood" (song by Raffi) or "Sit Down, Stand Up Song" (song by Rick Goldin). I always end with "I'm in the mood for reading" or "Stand up if you like elephant and piggie," and then go into reading books.

One of my favorite imaginative play sessions is to read a space book, like *Zoom Zoom Zoom, I'm Off to the Moon* by Dan Yaccarino (Scholastic Press 1997), and then pretend to put on the gear, get in a rocket ship, and go into space. We have gone to Mars and the Moon, and we've also skipped in-between planets. We've walked with no gravity and collected moon rocks, some big and some small, and I've asked my favorite question: "Do we see anything now that we are on Mars?" We have seen aliens, some scary and some not so much, and even a fairy princess.

Then I bring my guitar back out to transition back to sitting. We will sing a song or do a story on the guitar, read a few more books, and then we sing a goodbye song. And of course, if we have time, I always let every child come up and play the guitar.

## PRESCHOOL STORYTIMES FOR THE LIBRARY

Because of my experience in my preschool, doing preschool visits for the library is somewhat easy. I do a storytime very similarly, but I always introduce myself as a librarian from the Boulder Public Library. I try to have a picture of the library and get the kids familiar with where the library is. (Especially for the older kids.) I talk about what the library has: books, movies, a fish tank, a big playground out front, and so on. After I've introduced myself,

I will bring out Larry or my guitar, and then we start reading some books. I have had many kids from preschools come into the library when I am working and say hello. And of course, most always ask, "Is Larry here? Can I see him?"

# WOMEN'S SHELTER VISITS

When I started at the library, before doing musical storytimes, we visited the women's shelter of Boulder County (Safehouse Progressive Alliance for Nonviolence) and presented storytimes once a week for the children staying there. I learned *so much* doing these visits. They were some of the hardest and yet most fulfilling storytimes I have ever done. I had to attend a training session to understand what these families were going through. I mainly saw mothers with small children who had recently left an abusive situation and were staying at the shelter until they could find other options. Sometimes I read to mothers and their children, and sometimes it was just the children. Sometimes it was 15 kids; sometimes it was 2. I learned quickly to never expect anything and to be open to reading to whoever wanted to listen. At first I wanted to read things that were popular, but I quickly learned some tips I would love to share here.

What worked best were not the popular books at all; they were the silly, fantastical books that made the kids laugh. A large part of it was about getting those kids to escape reality through a book. Even if it was just for 20 minutes, I really tried to get those kids to relax and laugh. Books that worked really well were books where the children felt superior to the main characters in the book. *The Dumb Bunnies* by Sue Denim (Blue Sky Press/Scholastic 1994) and all the books in that series were a huge success. The kids loved pointing out all the things the Dumb Bunnies are doing wrong. We would spend time on each page looking for silly things. Another thing I learned was that the books about real people did not work as well as the personified animal books. From what I understand, the situation at hand can trigger strong emotions when reading about real people. An example of this is David Shannon's *No David* (Blue Sky Press 1998). I thought this book was somewhat silly, and the story has a sweet resolution at the end, but he is being told "No" a lot, and I had a child get really scared while I was reading it. Search and Find books, such as *Where's Waldo* by Martin Handford (Candlewick Press 1997), work well with small groups. But know where things are located so you can help find them if the children are getting frustrated.

Here are some other books that worked well:

Fieffer, Jules. *Bark George*
Micklethwait, Lucy. *I Spy a Freight Train: Transportation in Art*
Micklethwait, Lucy. *I Spy a Lion: Animals in Art*
Most, Bernard. *Cock-a-Doodle-Moo!*
Most, Bernard. *The Cow That Went Oink*
Stoke, Janet Morgan. *Minerva Louise*
Stoke, Janet Morgan. *Minerva Louise and the Red Truck*

# RECREATION CENTER VISITS

Boulder Public Library is a city entity. One of our city values is "collaboration." Our parks and rec department help us with summer reading events, and in turn we do storytimes for their summer camps. Doing storytimes at a recreation center is *very* different from doing it at a library setting. Groups can be big or small, and you really need to be prepped for all ages. The kids are usually put in two groups: (1) kindergarten to 2nd grade and (2) 3rd to 5th grade. Both these groups are a wide age range for reading. Sometimes they group them all together. That's extra fun! (Cough cough.) Also, it can be very difficult to read to group of kids who have just finished swimming and want to go back to the pool or shoot hoops in the gym. But here are some tips I have learned:

> Definitely bring an instrument, if you can. "Silly Dance Contest" (Jim Gill) and "Sit Down Stand Up Song" (Rick Goldin) work really well for all ages. And to give it a literacy edge, I will sing, "Stand up if you like Elephant and Piggie. Then sit back down. Stand up if you know who Jack and Annie are, and sit back down."
>
> I always bring a variety of books. With older kids, I mainly do book talks and/or read a short story. For younger kids, I will do picture books along with some movement like the Jellyfish and Form the Banana.
>
> People ask about crafts with big groups such as this. I am not a crafty person, but I like to bring in people who can do them. We have library volunteers to help with crafts. Once I was partnered with a craft, and that worked very well at a recreation storytime. The kids were given boondoggles, if they wanted, and most sat and weaved while I was reading to them.

# RECREATION CENTER VISITS AT PARKS (OUTSIDE)

I have done only a handful of visits like this, but I have learned a lot. First of all, have a microphone. Even just for reading stories, a mic will help tremendously. We have a small amplifier that hooks up to a small speaker, and it works really well. You just have to make sure that the organizer knows you will need electricity. Choosing books for these storytimes is always tricky. I try to go for popular/current books that have a wide appeal.

Here are books that have worked well:

Daywalt, Drew. *The Legend of Rock Paper Scissors*

Klassen, Jon. *Sam and Dave Dig a Hole*

Lubar, David. *Invasion of the Road Weenies* (This is a collection of short stories and works better for older kids. "Copies" is *hilarious*!)

Novak, B. J. *Book with No Pictures* (This book works *amazingly* to make kids laugh and really works well with all ages. But prep it! It's a performance piece.)

O'Malley, Kevin. *Once upon a Cool Motorcycle Dude*

Thomson, Bill. *Chalk* (Talk about this when you're done, and have the kids talk about what they would draw if they had magic chalk.)

Willems, Mo. *There Is a Bird on Your Head* (I really like just about all the Elephant and Piggie books. These can also work on getting a parent involved and having them, or an older child, play one of the voices.)

# BIRTHDAY STORYTIMES

Once I started using instruments, I received quite a few requests to do birthday storytimes. I had done library birthday storytimes, where I actually got paid as a librarian, and it was a side program in the library. But they did not work well due to the nature of 10–20 kids running around eating cake and excited to open presents. I asked my boss about the said request, which was to go to someone else's home and do a storytime as an entertainer, for money. My boss asked our administration, and I got the okay. We figured it was a side/contracted job and as long as I specified that it was not connected to the library, it would work. I still do them today. I never use library materials, unless I have checked them out as a regular patron. I bring my own guitar and have some flannels and puppets, and so on.

The main thing I have learned from doing these storytimes is that to make it a success, make it very special for the child having the birthday. I work very closely with the person giving the party and find out what the child's favorite stories are, including songs and flannels, and so on. I let the child help me with the actual storytime, if he or she is willing. This is something I have never done in my regular storytimes. During my library storytime I am the only one who touches the books, flannels, and so on, and at the end I *always* let everyone play with all the materials I have used during the storytime. But for a birthday, I let the birthday child be the main focus! If they want to do the entire flannel, I let them put the whole thing up while I am telling the story. They *love* that! There have been a few times when they are scared or overwhelmed, but in that case I ask the child if everyone can help (since it is usually a small group), or I just do the story.

So to reiterate, the most important thing is to work with the person giving the party to create a script you know the birthday child will love.

One of my favorite birthday storytimes was book-themed. It was for a little girl turning three. The organizer had books corresponding with all the food. She had *Very Hungry Caterpillar* by Eric Carle (Penguin 1969) next to a bowl of gummy worms and *One Fish Two Fish Red Fish Blue Fish* by Dr. Seuss (Random House 1960) next to a bowl of colored goldfish crackers. The birthday cake was based on *Chicka Chicka Boom Boom* by Bill Martin (Simon and Schuster 1989). It was adorable! For the actual storytime, I did an opening song on the guitar and then read all the child's favorites. Then we did one of her favorite flannels, and she put all the pieces up herself. Then we did some dancing with the guitar, and we were done! It was so fun! They had pizza, and then all the partygoers got a book to take home.

Another birthday storytime was bear-themed. The little boy turning four loved bears. I did bear books and then we ended with a flannel version of *We're Going on a Bear Hunt* based on the book by Michael Rosen. He *loved* that story so much we ended up going on a bear hunt throughout his entire house. It was hilarious. The kids actually ran outside, ran in the door, and ran to his bed, and all got under his covers.

One of my favorite birthday storytimes was for a baby turning one. I was apprehensive when asked, because first of all, it was for a baby, and second, they wanted to have it at a park, which hardly ever works for me. Competing with slides and a climbing gym is hard. (See Recreation Center Storytimes.) But I worked with the mother, and, really—the birthday party was kind of for her too, because that one year mark is huge for a first-time mother! (I remember it well!) She told me the child's favorite songs and that the baby loved scarves and instruments.

Mother set up a beautiful section underneath a big shady tree with blankets. It was just far enough away from the playground that it worked. That beautiful mother sat with the baby in her lap while I played the guitar, and we sang "Twinkle Twinkle Little Star" and "Itsy Bitsy Spider." Then I read *On the Day You Were Born* by Debra Frasier (Harcourt Inc. 1991) for the adults and *Pete the Cat: I Love My White Shoes* by Eric Litwin (Harper. 2008) for the kids. We talked about colors, and then got out scarves, and the kids ran around throwing them in the air while I sang "Teddy Bear's Picnic" (based on the song version by Jerry Garcia). I can't remember exactly which songs, but I played a couple more, and we were done. It was wonderful.

I would also like to mention our television program, *Read with Us*, which I talk about in Chapter 5 "Themed Storytimes and Scripts." Although it is not necessarily live outreach, it is a form of outreach and a way we have taken our storytimes to a much broader audience. We are in our second season and learning so much about copyright and literacy performance on a smaller level. Nevertheless, the main thing I have learned from my outreach experience is how necessary it is to build a stronger community. Outreach is simply defined as "to surpass in reach" (https://www.merriam-webster.com). It's to take what we offer at the library to a wider audience. Not only does this better our community, but it also has made my life richer. I love going to preschools as "Ms. Melanie the Librarian." As if being a librarian is my superpower. But I've also been deeply affected by the children at the women's shelter and the kids just wanting to play ball at the rec centers (but will totally get into a story or song). Outreach has made me better understand the impact I have on our community. That may sound a little selfish, but what I learn every time I go out is it's not just all about the library. It's the impact we are making on a person's life. I compare using a guitar in storytime to a rock concert. To that first time you hear a song live and how thrilling it is. I swear, taking storytime on the road is similar. Not necessarily thrilling, but to a child that act of you thinking they are important enough that you come to them is huge. I have seen it. With my guitar in hand and my bag of books by my side I'm off to bring literacy to the world! (Or so it feels.)

## ALBUMS AND SONGS

Garcia, Jerry and David Grisman. *Not for Kids Only*. Acoustic Disc. 1993. "Teddy Bear's Picnic."
Gill, Jim. *Jim Gill Sings the Sneezing Song and Other Contagious Tunes*. Jim Gill Music. 1993. "Silly Dance Contest."
Goldin, Rick. *I Like to Read*. CD Baby. 2012. "Sit Down Stand Up."
Raffi. *Rise and Shine*. Rounder Records. 1996. "I'm in the Mood."

# BOOKS

Barnett, Mac, and Jon Klassen. *Sam and Dave Dig a Hole*. Somerville, MA: Candlewick Press, 2014.
Carle, Eric. *Very Hungry Caterpillar*. New York: Penguin Putnam Books for Young Readers, 1969.
Daywalt, Drew, and Adam Rex. *The Legend of Rock Paper Scissors*. New York: Balzer & Bray, 2017.
Denim, Sue, and Dav Pilkey. *The Dumb Bunnies*. New York: Blue Sky Press/Scholastic, 1994.
Fieffer, Jules. *Bark George*. New York: HarperCollins, 1999.
Frasier, Debra. *On the Day You Were Born*. Orlando, FL: Harcourt Inc., 1991.
Handford, Martin. *Where's Waldo?* Somerville, MA: Candlewick Press, 1997.
Litwin, Eric. *The Nuts: Sing and Dance in Your Polka Dot Pants*. New York: Little, Brown and Company, Inc., 2015.
Lubar, David. *Invasion of the Road Weenies*. New York: Tor Books, 2006.
Martin, Bill, Jr., and John Archambault. *Chicka Chicka Boom Boom*. Illustrated by Lois Ehlert. New York: Simon and Schuster Books for Young Readers, 1989.
Micklethwait, Lucy. *I Spy a Freight Train: Transportation in Art*. New York: Greenwillow Books, 1996.
Micklethwait, Lucy. *I Spy a Lion: Animals in Art*. New York: Greenwillow Books, 1994.
Most, Bernard. *Cock-a-Doodle-Moo!* San Diego: Harcourt Brace & Co., 1996.
Most, Bernard. *The Cow That Went Oink*. Orlando, FL: Harcourt Inc., 1990.
Novak, B. J. *Book with No Pictures*. New York: Dial Books, Penguin, 2014.
O'Malley, Kevin, Carol Heyer, and Scott Goto. *Once upon a Cool Motorcycle Dude*. New York: Walker & Co., 2005.
Rosen, Michael, and Helen Oxenbury (eds.). *We're Going on a Bear Hunt*. New York: Macmillan Publishing Company, 2005.
Seuss, Dr. *One Fish Two Fish Red Fish Blue Fish*. New York: Random House Inc., 1960.
Shannon, David. *No, David*. New York: Blue Sky Press, 1998.
Stoeke, Janet Morgan. *Minerva Louise*. New York: Penguin Young Readers, 1993.
Stoeke, Janet Morgan. *Minerva Louise and the Red Truck*. New York: Dutton Children's Books, 2002.
Thomson, Bill. *Chalk*. Tarrytown, New York: Marshall Cavendish, 2010.
Udry, Janice May. *A Tree Is Nice*. Illustrated by Marc Simont. New York: Harper & Row, 1987.
Willems, Mo. *There Is a Bird on Your Head!* Willems, MO: Hyperion, 2007.
Yaccarino, Dan. *Zoom Zoom Zoom, I'm Off to the Moon*. New York: Scholastic Inc., 1997.

# Conclusion

Now that the book is finished, what have we learned? Here are our thoughts.

After the initial excitement of being asked to write a book wore off, the first hurdle was choosing a title. That was tricky. It's sort of like naming a baby . . . you don't really know if they will grow gracefully into their name. There's no field on the birth certificate to pencil in "working title." Fortunately, we got lucky. Our baby, *Storytime and Beyond: Having Fun with Early Literacy*, has turned out just the way we had hoped.

Storytime is the foundation for early literacy in a library, and Melanie and I both have excellent storytime experience, which we've detailed. But it's the "beyond" idea that we've also described, including outreach and training sessions for parents and caregivers.

Having fun is at the core of meaningful learning, and we've stressed that. One of my early mentors gave me some excellent career advice when she said, "If it's not *fun*, don't do it!" I kept that in mind, and when she finally retired many years later, I asked if she had any regrets about leaving the job. "Not really," she said, "it stopped being *fun*." Luckily for me, the fun never stopped, and I've been thrilled to be able to pass it along in my chapters.

We are delighted with the cover of our book. Early on, we had been given the opportunity to submit ideas. We suggested that alphabet letters and musical notes should be prominent, mentioned that the title should be visible from across the room, and the whole thing should convey *fun.* Less than a month before our final deadline, we saw the cover and loved it!

I've tried to keep in mind the dual concept of books: they can be mirrors and/or windows. The reader should be able to see something of his or her own reflection in the words and pictures. And/or, the reader should get a glimpse into world outside his or her own. Our cover is a mirror of our experiences, and the book itself is a window (beyond . . .) into the fun to be had with early literacy.

The little bird on the cover was a surprise. I see it as a symbol of our book "leaving the nest," and spreading fun.

—Kathy

That's funny, because I saw the bird and thought of "Three Little Birds" a song by Bob Marley. And I must say, I am *so thankful* to have been able to write this book with Kathy and our helpful editor, Jessica. Both were calming voices whispering (or even singing!) to me while I wrote.

As much fun it is to do Musical Storytime, writing about it has been much harder than anticipated! I know it sounds cliché, but it was difficult for me to put in writing something that has come so easily for me. Especially the fact that my storytimes change so much year to year. Writing down a script, or a certain way to present a storytime, felt so *final.* I feel the need to write a BLOG to keep the ideas I learned from the book and continue to learn from the day-to-day implication of storytime. Recently I had a coworker come to me with a brand new ukulele and ask me, "Ok, what do I do next?" My heart dropped, and I was thinking, "Did I put that in the book?" But then I remember the bird on the book. We went to YouTube, as I suggest in the book, and the first video that came was a perfect step-by-step instruction video on how to play the ukulele. *Whew.*

But what have I learned? I've learned to trust the process of being a storyteller. No storyteller is better than the other; we are just different. I must piggyback on what Kathy says and really reiterate: make sure you have an element of fun in everything you do and adjust to your passion, whether it be ABC books, displays, or a particular storytime style. The resources are out there; you just need to know where to look. We hope this book will be a very good place to start.

—Melanie

# Index

# About the Authors

KATHY BARCO is a freelance library consultant following her retirement as literacy coordinator at Albuquerque/Bernalillo County Library System. She was a children's librarian with the ABC Library and served five years as youth services coordinator for the New Mexico State Library. She earned her MLIS from the University of Southern Mississippi, Hattiesburg, Mississippi. She received the Leadership Award from the New Mexico Library Association in 2006. She served two terms on the board of the New Mexico Library Foundation. She is a member of the New Mexico Library Association, the Mountain Plains Library Association, and American Library Association (ALA). Barco has coauthored three books with Valerie Nye: *True Stories of Censorship Battles in America's Libraries* (2012), *Breakfast Santa Fe Style*, and *Breakfast New Mexico Style* (2006, 2009). Kathy's book *READiscover New Mexico: A Tri-Lingual Adventure in Literacy* (2007) won a 2008 New Mexico Book Award.

MELANIE BORSKI-HOWARD has been working in bookstores and libraries for over 25 years. She currently works at the Boulder Public Library as a youth services specialist. She has been reading stories to children for over 15 years and currently presents four to five storytimes per week. She has also taught creative writing to teens and run several library programs. Her on-demand storytime show, *Read with Us*, is in its second season on the local TV Channel 8 in Boulder, Colorado. Melanie is a member of the Colorado Library Association and CLEL (Colorado Libraries for Early Literacy).